OVERCOMING DEPRESSION

■

A Cognitive-Behavior
Protocol for the
Treatment of Depression

Gary Emery, Ph.D.

Distributed in the U.S.A. by Publishers Group West; in Canada by Raincoast Books; in Great Britain by Airlift Book Company, Ltd.; in South Africa by Real Books, Ltd.; in Australia by Boobook; and in New Zealand by Tandem Press.

Copyright © 2000 by Gary Emery
     New Harbinger Publications, Inc.
     5674 Shattuck Avenue
     Oakland, CA 94609

Cover design by Poulson/Gluck Design
Edited by Carole Honeychurch
Text design by Michele Waters

ISBN 1-57224-161-6 Paperback

New Harbinger Publications' Web site address: www.newharbinger.com

02 01

10 9 8 7 6 5 4 3

Contents

Introduction: Depression — A Brief Overview

What We Know About Depression

The current system of defining depression is descriptive. Researchers define depression by your symptoms—how you think, feel, and act. The descriptive method makes it easier for professionals to agree, and allows for an effective way to define the disorder.

Depression is a group of enduring symptoms that last anywhere from a few weeks to years. Symptoms are broken down into four clusters: how you think (a negative view of the self, the world, and the future), how your body reacts (trouble with sleep and/or your appetite), how you act (slowed down, apathetic), and how you feel (sad, guilty, anxious).

Depression can develop rapidly or come on slowly over a period of weeks. Some depressions are mild; you're able to go through your normal steps but you feel bad and lack energy. At other times, you may become so depressed and suicidal that you need hospitalization.

A negative state of mind that colors all of your experiences is the chief feature of depression. You may cry a great deal; or even worse, you want to cry but can't. Simple chores require great effort and everyday problems seem overwhelming. You become your own worse critic and believe that you're being punished for something you did wrong.

This disorder is not only debilitating but can be a significant health problem. The lifetime risk for women is 10 percent to 25 percent and 5 percent to 12 percent for men. Suicide, a byproduct of depression, is a leading cause of death (American

Psychiatric Association, Washington D.C. 1994). Research has found worldwide one percent to 4 percent of adults state they have attempted suicide (Jamison 1999).

You might see depression as somewhat paradoxical: You may seek punishment, humiliation, and death no matter how much achievement and social success you have. Yet the chances for recovery are excellent, and complete remission of an episode of depression occurs in up to 95 percent of cases.

Criteria for Depression

You can be considered depressed if you can answer yes to two broad questions: Have you had a distinct period of feeling unhappy or a distinct period of overall loss of pleasure and interest? Have you suffered from five of the following eight symptoms for at least two weeks?

- appetite or weight change
- sleep problems
- excessive tiredness
- physically slowed down or agitated
- a loss of interest or pleasure in usual activities
- feeling guilty
- slow thinking or indecisiveness
- thoughts of killing yourself

You can use these two questions as a guide to discover whether you are depressed or not.

Cause of Depression

The most likely explanation of depression is that it is a built-in, natural response to feeling defeated. From an evolutionary perspective, depression allows you to shut down until the dire conditions improve. Every human, if they feel defeated enough, will become depressed.

When you become depressed, your mind and body are operating exactly as they were designed to do when faced with insurmountable obstacles. The problem is that you are reacting to an imagined total defeat, rather than a real one. In other words, the obstacles aren't actually insurmountable—you just perceive them that way.

Most people muddle through their depression the best they can. Because depression usually is self-limiting, your depression will likely lift—although this may take a while. Fortunately, you can do more than just wait. You have a choice of a range of effective treatments for depression. You can learn to overcome your depression and help prevent future depressions.

What We Know About Treating Depression

Medical Treatment Approaches

Indirect Medical Treatments

Different physical problems—among them infections, cancer, epilepsy, vitamin deficiencies, some forms of arthritis, and disorders of the endocrine system—are associated with symptoms of depression. Here, the depression symptoms are secondary to the physical problems. Generally, if you medically treat the physical problems, the depression will clear up.

Similarly, side effects of some drugs may be the real problem. Antihypertension drugs, cardiac drugs, acne drugs, birth control pills, and steroids, among others, can bring on the depression syndrome. If safe to do so, the removal or change of drugs will clear up the depression. For these reasons, if you suffer from depression, you should have a physical examination and have any current medications you're taking checked out for depressive side effects.

Electric Shock Therapy (EST)

Although once used extensively to treat depression, EST is used much less now. No one knows quite why EST works, but it can dramatically help some cases. EST is used mainly as a last resort, when other treatments haven't worked or when the person is an extreme suicide risk.

Bipolar Drugs

Bipolar depression, characterized by fluctuating periods of mania, is the one form of depression best treated with drugs. The disorder, which affects only a small portion of depressed people, is believed to be inherited, and is often triggered by stress. Drugs such as lithium can control this disorder, but since there seems to be a psychological as well as a physical component to the problem, the best treatment is often a combination of drugs and psychotherapy.

Antidepressants

The new anti-depressants have become an increasingly popular form of treatment. Although they are widely prescribed, their degree of effectiveness is questionable. In the few controlled studies done to date, they have been found to be only slightly more effective than placebos (Schiffer 1998).

Anti-depressant drugs have side effects, such as drowsiness, dizziness, dry mouth, and loss of sexual interest. Older people in particular are sensitive to the side effects. Others with certain physical problems such as hypertension can't take the drugs. Although drugs may work quicker than psychotherapy, relapse rates are higher for those who only take drugs to overcome depression.

A number of research projects studying the effectiveness of cognitive behavior therapy, the treatment this program uses, have found that the vast majority of people can overcome their depression without drugs. They have also been found to have much lower relapse rates than people treated with drugs (DeRubeis 1998).

Psychological Treatment Approach

Psychological (as opposed to medical) therapy is the other major form of treatment for depression. Despite the differences among the range of therapies available, they can be broken down into insight and cognitive-behavior therapy.

Insight Therapy

The goal of traditional insight therapy is to help you understand the source of your problems. The type of understanding depends on the therapy. In analytic therapy, the focus is on understanding the early childhood traumas that are believed to cause your depression. One theory is that when you're depressed, you're actually really angry at someone else. Because you can't express this anger, you turn it inward and become depressed. Another approach is to provide insight into your significant relationships. Good relationships are a significant buffer against depression.

Cognitive-Behavior Therapy

This program uses a form of cognitive-behavior therapy. This form of therapy is an educational approach that focuses on present concerns. It is more interested in correcting the causes that maintain your depression, rather than in finding original causes. Like traditional insight therapies, it unearths dysfunctional beliefs that predispose you to depression. Cognitive-behavior therapy, however, places more emphasis on learning how to master your internal world of thoughts, feelings, and motivation.

The basic principle of this approach is: *How you think about your experiences determines how you react emotionally.* Each thought determines your momentary experience of reality, and because there is no limit to how many times you can have a specific thought, you can keep a depression going for a long time. If you think you're in danger of losing something you need, you'll feel anxious; if you think others have taken away something you need, you'll feel angry; if you think you've permanently lost something you need to be happy, you'll become depressed. When you become depressed, you systematically distort your experiences in a negative direction. You see yourself as a loser and your problems as too difficult to overcome.

More About This Treatment Approach

This treatment for overcoming your depression will take place over ten weekly sessions. Here is a brief outline:

1. Initial evaluation,

2. Understanding depression,

3. Master behavioral symptoms,

4. Taking action on procrastination,

5. Mastering feeling symptoms,

6. Challenging negative thoughts,

7. Mastering thinking symptoms,

8. Challenging beliefs,

9. Practice,

10. Review, closure, and planning follow-up.

Ten weekly sessions is the minimum time needed to learn and practice the skills. You may need more than ten weeks to fully grasp the ideas and skills; however, you will have learned enough that by the end of ten weeks you can continue on your own, if necessary. Your therapist may continue to work with you beyond ten sessions. If this is impractical, the therapist will be available by phone if you need assistance.

As you can see, the treatment approach is highly practical. Your therapist will not spend much time exploring your past. Research has demonstrated that such an approach is not particularly helpful with depression. Instead, you will learn skills and strategies that enable you to learn more adaptive ways of thinking, feeling, and acting. The term for this treatment approach is cognitive-behavior therapy. This approach is one of the major forms of psychological treatment for depression.

Schedule

The outline above explains the progression of treatment. During the first session, to tailor the therapy specifically to you, your therapist will do a thorough evaluation of your situation. In session 2, you will learn what role negative thinking plays in your depression. You will learn about the skills to get undepressed. If you practice these skills, you will learn to tell when you have slipped into a negative orientation and how to reverse out of it.

Session 3 focuses on how to counter the cognitive distortions that lead you to assume you are defeated by taking a proactive steps toward getting active.

In session 4, you will learn to tackle difficult tasks you have been putting off by breaking them down into manageable steps.

In session 5, you will learn how to use thought records to detect errors in your thinking. You will learn to spot the three cognitive (or thought) errors of depression.

Session 6 teaches you how to answer the thoughts that keep you depressed. This includes what action you can take.

In session 7, you will learn how to catch and drop thoughts (negative thinking) that lock you into depression. One of the chief features of being human is the tendency to create theories and then find evidence to support them. This tendency becomes a major problem when you are depressed. You convince yourself that you are helpless and hopeless. With practice you learn to quickly drop negative stories before they gain a foothold.

Session 8 focuses on the dysfunctional beliefs that make you vulnerable to depression. In this session, you will learn how absolute beliefs about important issues such as love, health, security, attractiveness, social status, and career success can set you up for depression.

Session 9 deals with remaining issues and practicing the skills you have learned.

In Session 10, you will sum up what you have learned and plan your follow-up.

The heart of the program is the real-life practice of the skills and new understanding you will gain. Throughout therapy, your therapist will coach you in the new skills you'll be learning, helping you put your new concepts in to practice. You will be able to get feedback on how you are doing and what you can do to improve.

The Goals of Treatment

Through practicing the skills taught, you will be able to get undepressed and learn how to prevent future depression. This goal includes two components: 1) You will be free of the symptoms of depression, and 2) you will have gained the understanding and skills to avoid future depressions.

These components mean that by the end of treatment you will feel better, have more energy, will be more connected to life, will be able to concentrate and think better, and will no longer avoid what needs to be done. You will be able to use the acquired skills in the daily stress you encounter.

You're not expected to totally master all of the skills and concepts. You will, however, have a blueprint for how to practice and gain greater mastery over your own psychology.

Self-Rating Scales

The treatment uses two scales that help you and your therapist assess the severity of your depression. The first one is the Center for Epidemiologic Studies Depressed Mood Scale (CES-D), which you'll complete during your first, fifth, and tenth sessions. Weekly, you'll complete the Depression Questionaire, which provides an up-to-the-minute gauge for your symptoms of depression. Both measures are reproduced in your client manual in the appropriate sessions.

Homework

Since cognitive-behavior therapy is an educational approach, you'll be asked to practice skills between sessions. At the end of each session, your therapist will give you a homework assignment. For example, after the second week you will be asked to practice a strategy of self-monitoring. During later sessions, you will practice other skills, not only during therapy sessions but on your own. You should bring your client manual to each session so your therapist can review your progress.

As you can see, your success with this therapy program *depends* on your commitment to do weekly homework assignments. Each week, at the beginning of the session, your therapist will review how the previous week's homework went and help you with any problems that come up. If something gets in the way of your doing the homework, you and your therapist will explore why and then be able to make adjustments.

Commitment

What you put into this therapy program is what you'll get out of it. You are more likely to overcome your depression faster if you do the assignments. If you do not make the time, you will get less out of the program, so it's important for you to evaluate your own level of commitment at the outset. The homework assignments require no more time and effort than a typical course in high school—they'll be easy to complete if you have the willingness to do so.

If you feel ready to make and sustain that kind of commitment, you are ready to undertake cognitive-behavior therapy. If you are not ready right now, it would be wise to begin the program at a later time. It's important that you discuss any concerns you have about doing homework assignments with your therapist during the first two or three sessions.

Session 1

Initial Evaluation

You have probably already completed the first session, in which your therapist asked you a number of questions about the history and background of your depression, how you have coped with it to date and what, if any, types of help you have sought. You also should have received a brief explanation of the therapy program, similar to what was described in the previous section, "About This Treatment Program." Your therapist should have answered any questions you have about the treatment during the first session. If not, be sure to bring them up next time. Finally, you probably completed two short self-examinations, the Depression Questionaire and the CES-D, both of which rate, the intensity of your symptoms. You will take the Depression Questionaire at the beginning of each session as a way to check in with your state of mind. The CES-D will be repeated in the fifth and in the final session as a broader gauge of your depression.

The nine remaining chapters in this book contain descriptions of the various concepts and skills you will learn to help you overcome your depression. Read the material for each session carefully to reinforce what you learn each week in therapy. If you have any questions about the concepts and skills, bring them up the following session. At the end of each session, you'll find a homework assignment that matches the one you'll receive from your therapist.

The Action Schedule

In this program, you will use two basic tools: 1) the action schedule, and 2) the thought record. Your therapist will go over the action schedule first. You'll see completed and blank action schedules at the end of this chapter. This is an hour-by-hour schedule of your week, going from 9 A.M. to midnight.

The action schedule is a simple-looking form and you may be wondering what it has to do with getting over your depression. When you systematically use the action schedule, it becomes a powerful tool in helping you get undepressed.

One of the ideas this program stresses is that you want to collect information or facts to see if your thoughts are true or not. The action schedule is the best way to gather this information.

Remember, the major feature of depression is that you systematically distort your experiences in a negative direction. You have an overall unrealistic negative picture of yourself, your world, and your future. You make three major thinking errors: 1) You think the implications of a negative event will go on forever, 2) that it will spread to all areas of your life, and 3) that you are to blame because of some inherent fault. You see yourself as a loser in all areas of your life, for all time. Because you believe this, you become depressed. Feelings of total defeat logically follow from these misperceptions. If you think you're doomed and you'll always be doomed, it's logical that you'd feel depressed.

It's not productive to argue with depressed people as to whether their perceptions are true or not. In the same vein, it's not productive to argue with yourself. If you didn't believe these three negative conclusions to some extent, you wouldn't be depressed, and it's often futile to try to argue anyone out of a belief. It's much more useful to look at these negative notions as possibilities that need to be checked out. Some negative thoughts may, in fact, be true. But because when you're depressed you have so many more false ones than true ones, you'll need to throw some light on the subject—by gathering the facts.

One of the best ways to do this is with an action schedule. The action schedule has a number of uses in getting undepressed. The first one is to collect information to see if your thoughts and beliefs reflect reality or whether they reflect the distorted thinking that keeps you depressed.

You may believe that you aren't accomplishing anything during the day or that you don't find enjoyment in anything. When you tell yourself this, rather than argue with yourself, test the idea out by using the action schedule. You do this by recording, on an hourly basis, what you're doing and your sense of mastery and pleasure from the activity. You can then really see if you're overlooking mastery and pleasure experiences and thinking in all-or-none terms about your future, your life, and yourself.

For example, you may think that you aren't doing any work. When you look at your weekly record sheet, you'll probably see that, in fact, you are doing some work. Seeing facts will make you feel better and give you motivation to start other things you may be putting off.

In the same way, you may think you have no enjoyment in the things you do. If you believe that you get no enjoyment, say, from being with other people, you'll probably prefer to be alone, isolating yourself. However, by looking at your action schedule, you may discover that you actually enjoy yourself with people and don't enjoy yourself as much when you're isolating yourself.

Your therapist will guide your practice of using the action schedule yourself using the sample action schedule as an initial example. On the sample, you notice that the person rated pleasure and mastery. Using the blank form for this week (at the end of this chapter), write down what you did today and next to each activity, rate how much mastery and pleasure you got from it. You rate this from 0 to 5. Mastery refers to your sense of achievement—how difficult was it for you to accomplish a given activity? You would rate 1 if the activity took little or no effort, 3 if it took moderate effort, and 5 if the activity was extremely hard to do. Remember, this rating is based on how you're feeling and acting right now, when you're depressed. When you're feeling normal, going to the grocery store may be a 1 in mastery, but when you're depressed, this can be a 5 because of the added effort it takes.

Also, next to each activity rate how much pleasure it gave you, with 1 being no pleasure and 5 being a great deal of pleasure.

By monitoring your activities, you'll have your hard data on what you're doing and achieving. You'll be able to challenge the belief that you're doing nothing. You may find out that you're more active and competent than you thought and that you're enjoying yourself more than you knew. Even if this isn't the case, you'll have a good idea of what's getting in your way.

Because it's important to keep good records, you should make sure to carry this schedule with you. You can fold it up and keep it in your pocket. Some people like to write in a small tablet, but it's much better to use the action schedule so you can write down what really happens immediately, before it can be clouded by negative thinking. Remember, when you're depressed, you notice and remember negative and unpleasant events more readily than you notice positive and pleasant ones. The good things that happen are blotted out by your global pessimism.

Steps in Activity Monitoring

1. Write down what you do on an hour-by-hour basis. If you couldn't get all of your activities into the little box, then you're trying to include too much ("got out of bed, brushed teeth, walked to kitchen"). But if you don't have something to write into the space, then you're doing it too globally ("morning ritual"). You want something in between ("got up; made and ate breakfast").

2. Rate how much pleasure or mastery you get from each activity—1 to 5. Remember, you're always doing something (reading a newspaper or magazine is an activity, so is going to bed, or staring out of the window). They may not be activities that give you satisfaction, but they are activities and so should be recorded.

You may have trouble remembering if an activity brought any sense of mastery or pleasure. For this reason, you should rate mastery and pleasure right after or as close after the activity as you can. Studies of depressed people find they discount or forget the pleasure and mastery experiences that they have. By rating how much mastery and pleasure you have immediately, you can counteract this tendency.

Homework

Homework for session 2 is as follows:

1. Fill one action schedule out for the week and rate each activity for mastery and pleasure.

2. Read session 2 in your manual.

Action Schedule

Note: Grade activities M for Mastery and P for Pleasure

	Monday	Tuesday	Wednesday	Thursday	Friday	Saturday	Sunday
9–10							
10–11							
11–12							
12–1							
1–2							
2–3							
3–4							
4–5							
5–6							
6–7							
7–8							
8–12							

Action Schedule

Note: Grade activities M for Mastery and P for Pleasure

	Monday			Tuesday			Wednesday			Thursday	Friday	Saturday	Sunday	
9–10	Eat breakfast	M0 P2		Eat Breakfast	M0 P2		Go Shopping	M0 P1						
10–11	Do laundry	M2 P1		Run errands	M0 P0		Go shopping	M0 P2						
11–12	Watch T.V.	M0 P3		Watch T.V.	M0 P3		Meet friend	M0 P3						
12–1	Watch T.V. Eat lunch	M0 P3		Watch T.V. Eat lunch	M0 P3		Lunch with friend	M0 P3						
1–2	Go shopping	M4 P0		Go to doctor	M4 P0									
2–3	Take nap	M0 P3		Go to doctor	M4 P0									
3–4	Clean house	M3 P0		Clean house	M3 P0									
4–5	Fix dinner	M2 P0		Fix dinner	M2 P0									
5–6	Visit with family	M0 P3		Visit with family	M0 P3									
6–7	Eat & clean up	M4 P1		Eat & clean up	M4 P1									
7–8	Read paper	M0 P3		Attend meeting	M2 P1									

Center for Epidemiologic Studies Depressed Mood Scale (CES-D)

Using the scale below, indicate the number which best describes how often you felt, or behaved this way DURING THE PAST WEEK.

0 = Rarely or none of the time (less than 1 time)

1 = Some or a little of the time (1-2 days)

2 = Occasionally or a moderate amount of time (3-4 days)

3 = Most or all of the time (5-7 days)

DURING THE PAST WEEK

_____ 1. I was bothered by things that usually don't bother me.

_____ 2. I did not feel like eating; my appetite was poor.

_____ 3. I felt that I could not shake off the blues even with help from my family or friends.

_____ 4. I felt that I was just as good as other people.

_____ 5. I had trouble keeping my mind on what I was doing.

_____ 6. I felt depressed.

_____ 7. I felt that everything I did was an effort.

_____ 8. I felt hopeful about the future.

_____ 9. I thought my life had been a failure.

_____ 10. I felt fearful.

_____ 11. My sleep was restless.

_____ 12. I was happy.

_____ 13. I talked less than usual.

_____ 14. I felt lonely.

_____ 15. People were unfriendly.

_____ 16. I enjoyed life.

_____ 17. I had crying spells.

_____ 18. I felt sad.

_____ 19. I felt that people dislike me.

_____ 20. I could not get "going."

Depression Questionnaire

Choose a number from the scale below to show how much you are troubled by each problem listed. Write the number in the blank.

0	1	2	3	4	5	6	7	8
Hardly at all		Slightly troublesome		Definitely troublesome		Markedly troublesome		Very severely troublesome

_____ 1. Feeling miserable, empty, or depressed

_____ 2. Feeling bad about yourself

_____ 3. Feeling discouraged or hopeless about the future

_____ 4. Automatic negative thoughts coming into your mind

_____ 5. Feeling bad or discouraged about your life

_____ 6. Other feelings (describe) _____

_____ 7. How would you rate the present state of your depression symptoms on the scale below? Please circle one number between 0 and 8.

0	1	2	3	4	5	6	7	8
No symptoms present		Slightly disturbing/ not really disturbing		Definitely disturbing/ disabling		Markedly disturbing/ disabling		Very severely disturbing/ disabling

Weekly Practice Record

Goals for Week: Date:

1.

2.

3.

MON	TUES	WED	THUR	FRI	SAT	SUN

Session 2

Understanding Depression

The Negativity Factor

Like most people, you probably want to be happy, healthy, have good relationships, meaningful work, and creative outlets. But when you become depressed, you act contrary to what you normally want—you effectively reverse from a positive to a negative perspective. To understand this paradox, you need to realize that, generally, you have two separate ways of thinking—positively and negatively. Those prone to depression tend to switch easily and quickly into negative thinking. A major study at the University of Wisconsin found people that are high risk for depression react more strongly to negative events than those that are low risk for depression. The person vulnerable to depression believes 1) the negativity will go on forever, 2) it will spread to all areas of life, and 3) it is due to some personal fault.

Every depressed person is, to some degree, ambivalent about getting better: the positive side of you wants to, the negative side doesn't think it is possible, so why waste energy trying? The situation is similar to a person that wants to quit smoking, while at the same time, *doesn't* want to. This idea of dual ways of thinking explains why you may not want to take steps that you know will help you get undepressed.

You can recognize your negative thinking by noticing how negative and positive thoughts are phrased in your head. You generally use active language when you're thinking in a positive mode ("I can do it"), while more passive phrasing characterizes a switch to negativity ("Why does everything happen to me?"). Optimistic thinking takes the subject position and *acts* on the world. The less hopeful, depressive thinking takes the object position and feels acted *upon*.

Your state of mind determines your outlook on life. When you get depressed, you get stuck in the self-focused negative thinking. Because you're unable to see that life is a complex happening, you have difficulties detaching from thoughts and feelings. Your distorted view of reality makes life look too difficult, so you naturally feel small and vulnerable.

When you're depressed, you may bring a harsh parental voice to try to counter your sense of being defeated. This kind of self-talk, with its commands and imperatives, further deepens the depression.

"You need to get your act together."

"Yeah? Just try to make me."

"You'll do it."

"No. Never."

"You better."

"You can't make me do it."

The more you insist on what you should do, the more resistance you create. Rather than trying to force yourself out of depression using willpower, you need to gain an understanding of the nature of depression. In a depressed state of mind, you can always find evidence to support your belief that your situation is hopeless and action is useless. Once you get undepressed, you will be able to see your way around obstacles that previously seemed insurmountable.

All Problems and No Solutions

When you are depressed and happen to have a positive thought, feeling, or occurrence the tendency is to dismiss it and look for something negative to focus on. Because, in this state, you can see all the problems and none of the solutions, you believe answers don't exist. You feel hopeless and conclude that you are simply unable to get what you think you need. Because you are unable to get what seems imperative, you begin to shut off your desires altogether.

From an evolutionary perspective, negativity can be adaptive by providing the group with a clear view of what is wrong. False optimism can be detrimental when physical survival is at stake. If one were truly in a hopeless situation, shutting down until conditions improve would make sense.

Completely shutting down for an extended period of time, however, is rarely useful in modern life and is actually counterproductive. While it can be helpful to briefly see the full scope of the negative side, if negativity persists, you will become depressed. Depression is a backup evolutionary mechanism that may have been useful at one time in human evolution, but it's no longer needed to survive.

Reversal

Almost anything, from low blood sugar to everyday frustrations, can reverse you into negative thinking. Most of the time you'll quickly and automatically move back to the more balanced way of seeing things. When you're depressed, however, you stay in your defeated state of mind a disproportionate amount of time. What keeps you depressed is the belief that you need something you can't have. You may, for example, need the past to be different. Because you are convinced you cannot be happy without what you think you need, you begin to feel totally defeated.

Acceptance

You have a physical mechanism that automatically adjusts your physical movements. If you lose your balance and are about to fall, you automatically right yourself. Some people have a faulty mechanism and develop a disorder called "alien-hand syndrome." In this disorder, one hand does the opposite of the other—your left hand may slap and punch you, while your right hand tries to fend off this aggression.

This is similar to what happens to you when you get depressed. You fight against circumstances and against yourself. Because you can never win a fight with yourself, you end up defeated. Once depression takes over, you project negative thoughts about the past into the future, and you feel hopeless about the present.

When you're not depressed, you naturally switch back from negative to positive thinking. Normally it happens quickly, so you are not aware of how you switch from a negative to a positive outlook. In this therapy program, you will learn skills that will help you consciously switch out of the negativity so you can avoid future depressions.

You stay depressed when you are convinced you'll never be able to get what you think you need—what you believe you can't be happy without. This structural bind leads to the symptoms of depression. You then begin to need the depressive symptoms to be different, something you have been unable to achieve. This additional failure to get something that seems essential further strengthens the negative thinking's hold over you. In effect, you become depressed about being depressed. It is only when you accept the fact that you're suffering from depressive symptoms without dwelling on your perceived hopelessness that you can begin to override the depression by taking action.

"How" Questions

What keeps you dwelling on the negative is often "how" questions. When you ask yourself, "How can I do it," you can tend to over-focus on your negative, hopeless feelings. The best answer to "how" is "somehow." Asking yourself, "How can I avoid a loss in the future?" keeps you thinking about it. When you ask yourself, "How can I possibly get through this?" you reinforce the idea of suffering. You don't need to wonder how you will get out of your present bind. Better questions are "What do I want?" and "What do I need to do next?"

Turning Toward the Positive

Your negative side focuses exclusively on what you don't want (what you think needs to change) and not on what you do want. Your positive side is activated anytime you make a positive choice. You can always choose to think about what you would *like* to see happened. When you focus on what you want, your negative focus on what you don't want fades away.

Try to realize that reality is neutral, and that you can make the choice to think about any situation from a positive point of view. You can choose to see something as ugly or beautiful. You can choose to see risk as foolish or courageous. And choosing to get undepressed, in and of itself, is taking a turn toward the positive. You will not necessarily find good feelings immediately, but by deciding this is what you want you put forces into play that will lead to good feelings.

Taking Action

Depression is marked by passivity and self-absorption. You avoid doing what you perceive as too much work for too little reward. Your focus is turned in on yourself and you can lose contact with external reality. You replace common sense with private sense.

You can counter this by consciously taking action on present-moment needs. You do what needs to be done, no matter how difficult or easy it may seem. This means simply doing whatever comes next: washing the dishes, straightening the bedroom, calling a friend. Forget about the results—*simply taking the step is the victory*. Motivation comes after action. Conscious action is one of your most powerful tools when you get depressed.\When your focus turns inward, you lose perspective and blow small things up into big things. When you take action of any kind, you forget about your self for a while and activate your constructive mind.

You will use the action schedule to schedule actions that counteract your thoughts and feelings of negativity. For example, you can schedule fun actions that are incompatible with bad feelings. At the same time, you can tailor the actions to your needs. If you're lonely, you can schedule time with other people. If you're tense, you can schedule exercise or projects to get your mind off your tension.

Your motivation often works backward—once you do something you begin to feel like you want to do it more. Even if you have no desire to do a particular activity, if you jump in and start it, you'll probably discover that you *do* have some motivation. The action schedule helps you create this motivation. The more success you have in taking the actions on your action schedule, the more your motivation increases.

Homework

Homework for session 2 is as follows:

1. Fill out one action schedule this week and rate each activity for mastery and pleasure.

2. Read session 2 in the client manual.

Action Schedule

Note: Grade activities M for Mastery and P for Pleasure

	Monday	Tuesday	Wednesday	Thursday	Friday	Saturday	Sunday
9–10							
10–11							
11–12							
12–1							
1–2							
2–3							
3–4							
4–5							
5–6							
6–7							
7–8							
8–12							

Depression Questionnaire

Choose a number from the scale below to show how much you are troubled by each problem listed. Write the number in the blank.

0	1	2	3	4	5	6	7	8
Hardly at all		Slightly troublesome		Definitely troublesome		Markedly troublesome		Very severely troublesome

_____ 1. Feeling miserable, empty, or depressed

_____ 2. Feeling bad about yourself

_____ 3. Feeling discouraged or hopeless about the future

_____ 4. Automatic negative thoughts coming into your mind

_____ 5. Feeling bad or discouraged about your life

_____ 6. Other feelings (describe) _____

_____ 7. How would you rate the present state of your depression symptoms on the scale below? Please circle one number between 0 and 8.

0	1	2	3	4	5	6	7	8
No symptoms present		Slightly disturbing/ not really disturbing		Definitely disturbing/ disabling		Markedly disturbing/ disabling		Very severely disturbing/ disabling

Weekly Practice Record

Goals for Week: Date:

1.

2.

3.

MON	TUES	WED	THUR	FRI	SAT	SUN

Session 3

Mastering the Behavioral Symptoms

Questioning Your Predictions

Before you filled out the action schedule, what types of predictions did you make? ("I didn't enjoy myself at all"; "I didn't accomplish anything.") Now that you've filled out the activity schedule and you can see the facts, did these thoughts turn out to be true or exaggerations?

Some people's moods improve when they have mastery activity, while others find that pleasure activities are more helpful. Looking back on your moods, did you notice any difference in yourself? What makes you feel better—pleasure or mastery experiences?

Symptom Clusters

Remember, depression is an emotional disorder, a syndrome that is made up of a group of symptoms that continue over time. There are three major symptom clusters in depression: 1) how you act, 2) how you feel, and 3) how you think. A few symptoms of depression, such as problems with sleeping or appetite, are correlates with the other symptoms. That is, they're not directly caused by your thoughts, but show up attached to other symptoms of depression. For example, because you are in a defeated state of mind, your body goes into a shutdown mode. You have low energy and your appetites for food and sex are diminished. Keep in mind this idea of symptom clusters, because it provides an important clue to how you can get undepressed.

Mastering the First Cluster

Behavioral symptoms are the first cluster of symptoms you'll need to work on. They usually are the easiest to modify and when you correct them, you generally feel better and have more energy. They have to do with how you act when you're depressed, especially how slowed down and lethargic you can get. Getting yourself going may be difficult. You may put off tasks and let work pile up, or you may stop going out, spending more time at home lying around. You may start to think you've lost control over your life. Because everything has become so difficult and you feel so out of control, you may become excessively dependent upon others to solve your problems.

The best way to get over your depression is to translate your symptoms into challenges to master. Once you see them as challenges, you can focus on learning skills to master them. Then you can start to apply these ideas and skills to your specific situation, gaining a sense of control and mastery over what had previously defeated you.

Your Action Schedule

Depression is a pervasive disorder that can color all aspects of your life. As a result, it's difficult to get over your depression without working at it. You'll need to work within a systematic program and work on it on a daily basis.

The first step in this systematic program, and an effective way to tackle your behavioral symptoms is using the action schedule. Part of the nature of depression is that the structure in your life begins to deteriorate in the face of your low, lethargic feelings. Events just seem to happen. You don't seem to have any say over them. Scheduling your activities is a way to regain a sense of ownership of your life. Once you take charge of your time, you begin to be more effective in other areas of your life.

Because depression can undermine your will to get up and get things done, you may need a boost to help you do the tasks that keep your life moving. You may be avoiding chores or unpleasant tasks at work, but you may even find yourself resisting fun activities. Now you can use the action schedule to start scheduling more pleasurable activities like going to a movie, taking a walk, calling a friend, or spending some money on yourself. Even if they seem hard at first, once you commit to some specific activities by scheduling them, you're more likely to follow through.

You can also schedule mastery activities, such as jobs you've been putting off. Getting the car checked, filling out forms, or cleaning house may seem overwhelming, but when you schedule them and follow through, performing them one at a time, you'll discover that they weren't nearly as hard as you had assumed.

Try to schedule mastery and pleasure activities on a daily basis, either in the morning or at night. Write in what you're scheduled to do, then follow that schedule. You might tell yourself, "To get over my depression, I have to plan my work, then work my plan."

Remember to schedule routine activities, such as getting up, washing, and having breakfast. These may seem trivial, but when you're depressed they can be important sources of mastery. If it's difficult and yet you do it, give yourself a high mastery score.

Those who work diligently at scheduling their activities get over their depressions quicker. The more conscientious you are about it, the faster you'll feel good again.

By scheduling activities, you'll learn how to act when you don't feel like it. It takes effort to get undepressed. You learn anything new only through practice. You can't learn a skill in a classroom—you need to learn it in the context of where it will be used. You learn to swim in a swimming pool, not from a book or in a classroom. The same applies to learning to overcome depression. Immediately begin to use the techniques and continue to practice them until they become second nature. Although you don't need to keep completing action schedules throughout treatment, many people choose to continue using them.

At first, using the skill of scheduling activities may feel artificial and phony, but if you stick with it, it will eventually feel normal. By learning to act when you're unmotivated, you'll not only get over this depression, but you'll develop tools for avoiding future depressions as well.

Testing Your Negative Thoughts

A major benefit of scheduling activities is that you can find out what thoughts try to block you from doing an activity. The thoughts that block you often are the same ones that keep you depressed. You might think, "It's too hard"; "It's not worth the effort"; "I can't do it, why bother?" "It's too painful to think about."

By scheduling activities, you can also find out if this thinking is, in fact, accurate. This is important information. Testing these ideas out is crucial to overcoming your depression. You can test the ideas out by simply doing what's on the schedule and then you can reevaluate your ideas to see if they were true or not. At the end of each day, review your schedule and the activities you were able to accomplish. Try to recall what negative thoughts cropped up before you did each activity and evaluate whether these thoughts turned out to be true. Sometimes your negative thinking will be partially true, but most of the time you'll find that your activities were easier or more fun than you'd originally thought.

1. Schedule one or two days at a time, rather than a whole week. It is often helpful to schedule at night for the next day. Schedule on an hour-by-hour basis.

2. Be flexible in your scheduling. If an unexpected event occurs, you can change the schedule. Alternative plans can be made if the unexpected occurs.

3. If you don't do the scheduled action, it's not necessary to go back and make up what you missed. Rather, go ahead and continue with the action that you're doing. Don't ruminate over what you didn't do.

4. If you finish an action earlier than you planned (you finish the paper in thirty minutes rather than forty-five minutes), don't begin actions scheduled for later. Rather, do some fun or mastery action in the spare time. It helps to have a list to draw from of things you want to do and things you have to get done—constructive actions that don't take a lot of time, such as writing letters and reading magazines or newspapers.

5. You can use self-instruction about how you want to act to get moving. You may find talking to your muscles quite helpful ("Legs, get up out of the chair").

6. You can write instructions to yourself. You might write a script of how you plan to act, then follow the script. For example, you can say, "I'll jump out of bed, get dressed and out the door in thirty minutes, and be at work on time. I'll act friendly at work and be the first to say hello."

7. A general rule when you're depressed is not to lie down during the day. Force yourself to stay out of the bed and to remain upright, because reclining increases the feelings of depression and makes you more tired in the long run.

8. You may have some trouble in deciding what to schedule. In general, schedule actions around your normal routine. You can list typical ways you reacted before you got depressed and then try to perform these actions as if you were feeling fine.

9. When you plan actions, don't be too detailed ("Go down to the car, open the car door, get behind the wheel") or too general ("Go out for the day"). The goal is somewhere in between these two ("Go shopping downtown for a winter coat").

10. If you're having trouble finding pleasure actions to schedule, ask yourself questions such as, "What do I enjoy learning? What trips do I enjoy taking? What do I enjoy doing alone? What do I enjoy doing with others?" From these questions, you can generate a list of fun possibilities. Do the ones that have any glimmer of appeal for you.

11. To generate mastery actions, ask yourself similar questions. Once you've mad a list of mastery actions, you can arrange it in a hierarchy from easiest to most difficult. A mastery action is any activity you intend to do and then do. This can be as simple as putting on your clothes or driving to the store. Start by doing the easiest ones and then gradually increase the degree of difficulty.

12. Remember, the degree of mastery is subjective and is based on how you feel right now. When you're depressed, simple actions such as getting gas in the car may require a great deal of effort and thus deserve a high mas-

tery rating. When you're not depressed, they may not be mastery experiences at all. Use your current level of function as the judge.

13. Avoid grading your performance. Write down what you are going to do, not how much or how well you're going to do it.

14. After completing a scheduled day, reflect on what you did. This often provides a sense of mastery and helps in scheduling action for the following day.

Homework

Homework for session 3 is as follows:

1. Each day, schedule your activities for that day (you may want to schedule the night before).

2. Follow what is on the schedule. If you get behind, just focus on the next activity on the schedule.

3. Read session 3 in your manual.

Action Schedule

Note: Grade activities M for Mastery and P for Pleasure

	Monday	Tuesday	Wednesday	Thursday	Friday	Saturday	Sunday
9–10							
10–11							
11–12							
12–1							
1–2							
2–3							
3–4							
4–5							
5–6							
6–7							
7–8							
8–12							

Depression Questionnaire

Choose a number from the scale below to show how much you are troubled by each problem listed. Write the number in the blank.

0	1	2	3	4	5	6	7	8
Hardly at all		Slightly troublesome		Definitely troublesome		Markedly troublesome		Very severely troublesome

_____ 1. Feeling miserable, empty, or depressed

_____ 2. Feeling bad about yourself

_____ 3. Feeling discouraged or hopeless about the future

_____ 4. Automatic negative thoughts coming into your mind

_____ 5. Feeling bad or discouraged about your life

_____ 6. Other feelings (describe) _____

_____ 7. How would you rate the present state of your depression symptoms on the scale below? Please circle one number between 0 and 8.

0	1	2	3	4	5	6	7	8
No symptoms present		Slightly disturbing/ not really disturbing		Definitely disturbing/ disabling		Markedly disturbing/ disabling		Very severely disturbing/ disabling

Weekly Practice Record

Goals for Week: Date:

1.

2.

3.

MON	TUES	WED	THUR	FRI	SAT	SUN

Session 4

Taking Action on Procrastination

Why It's Complicated

When you're depressed, you feel guilt, apathy, fatigue, poor self-esteem, low mood, and have trouble with people. All of these symptoms can be countered by taking action on what you have been putting off. One of many paradoxes of depression is that you are extremely reluctant to put out any energy; however, when you take action, you feel better. You often fail to follow through on promises and obligations to others. This often makes you feel guilty, lowers your self-esteem, and causes others to reject you.

Why Bother?

You probably already know that you need to be more active on what you have been putting off. Friends and relatives may have urged and even harassed you about doing more. This, however, is seldom enough to motivate you.

When you feel defeated, you see little reason to invest any energy in something that has little possibility of return. In economic terms, when you're depressed, you don't believe you can win, you can only lose; so you don't want to invest. This can become a vicious cycle—the less you invest, the lower your return, which reinforces the notion that you can't win.

You can, however, interrupt this cycle of hopelessness and futility. When you can see the value of taking constructive action you will feel more ready to help bring about a success cycle.

Just as negative symptoms feed back and perpetuate your depression, you can get a positive feedback loop going the other way. Once you take action on what needs to be done, you generate positive feedback. This further motivates you to take more action and increases your sense of resourcefulness. You *show* yourself that you can start and complete projects, impressing yourself far more by action than you ever could by talk.

Because each mood has a corresponding state of mind, as your mood improves, so does your state of mind. Constructive action is the best way to raise your mood and overall outlook.

No matter how depressed you are, you will nearly always feel better after you become physically active. Researchers have found a simple, brisk ten-minute walk will raise your state of mind for several hours. Physical activity reduces body tension and shifts your focus off of your negative thoughts and feelings.

If you're still not convinced, take a look at the following advantages you'll gain by thwarting procrastination.

1. Taking action on avoidance moves you from where you are to where you want to be and raises your mood level.

2. Through directed action with specific targets, you gain mastery over your thinking and feelings. You choose the actions you want to take and you reinforce thoughts and feelings you want to have. By taking action, you program yourself for the experiences you want.

3. Action means you're sincere. Your mind gets the message that it's not just talk. Your action reinforces your commitment ("I am going to do what I have been avoiding") and build evidence that proves to yourself that you *can* overcome avoidance.

4. With each action against avoidance, you will find insights and new awareness that will help you continue moving forward.

5. You can create motivation by acting in accordance with a desired feeling or belief. Avoidance decreases motivation, action strengthens it.

6. Taking action on what you have been avoiding increases your focus, which in turn creates energy. Passivity drains energy. Taking action combats thoughts and feelings of helplessness. When you take action, you start to see you *can* get what you want.

7. Avoidance of what needs to be done to reach your goals creates body tension that drains energy and leads to fatigue. Once you confront the avoidance, you relax the tension and begin to feel physically better.

8. Taking action on what you have been avoiding is one of the best ways to get undepressed. By taking action, you stop negative thinking, focus outside of yourself, raise your mood, and expand your awareness.

Show, Don't Tell

When you're depressed, motivation works backwards. At first you're unmotivated; but, if you take action anyway, you *then* begin to feel motivated. Paradoxically, you only feel like taking action after you have already taken some. Make the aim not to do something, or have something, but simply to take action and see what happens next.

When you become depressed, your mental functioning drops. You have trouble concentrating, remembering, and learning. Because your brain does not believe it has any real, winnable challenges, it does not gear up.

You may have to master a real challenge by getting involved in reality. The best way to get your mental functioning back is to take action on what you have been avoiding. When you take on challenges, no matter how small, solutions to problems you once thought unsolvable start to appear.

Self-Approval

To get your own approval, what counts is what you do, not what you think or feel. If you do what needs to be done, you think well of yourself. The opposite often holds true when you avoid taking action. Your self-esteem takes a beating when you're depressed, because you put off what needs to be done.

Fortunately, you can regain your own self-approval relatively quickly. Simply start doing what you have been avoiding and then pay attention to how you feel about yourself. You'll discover that you start feeling better about yourself, and more able to take care of business.

After you have taken action, tune in to how you now think and feel about yourself. Give yourself credit, even if your depressed thinking wants to discount it. One of the reasons that you stay depressed is that, after you do something that is difficult, you minimize it. Make sure you reinforce your efforts at taking action.

Relativity

Remember, it's all relative. When you feel good, doing extremely difficult jobs may be easy and take little will or courage. However, when you are depressed, doing "easy" tasks can seem extremely difficult—so you should give yourself even more credit for doing them. To build momentum, notice how you really feel after you take action, giving credit where credit's due.

By becoming aware of the relationship between doing what needs to be done and how you feel about yourself, you will quickly realize that taking action is the means to self-esteem and meaning. When you do something that is difficult, you gain your own approval; when you fail to do this, you lose your own approval. If you like yourself, it doesn't matter what other people think about you. And if you don't like yourself, others' approval won't help.

Trouble with People

When you're depressed, you exaggerate how much other people don't like you. However, if you're like other depressed people, there may be a kernel of truth in this because depressed folks can be bad company. When you're depressed, you have little energy or will to be pleasant or generous with others, something friends may understand at first, but may grow tired of. After a while, people may begin to stay away from you if you remain depressed. Many people will be unhappy with your refusal to take action. Your lack of participation isolates you from others. You can only turn down so many invitations before people stop asking.

Your avoidance can cause real problems at work and with friends and relatives. When you are depressed, you tend not to keep promises and fail to follow through on agreements, which can upset and hurt others. Generally, you can rectify the situation by acknowledging your failure to follow through and correct the situation by taking action on what needs to be done.

People close to you could be the most upset by your passivity. They may begin to nag and even harass you about your lack of motivation. Unfortunately, this has the opposite effect when you are depressed: The more demands on you, the more oppositional you become. Others' displeasure with you causes you to feel worse about yourself and less motivated to take action. One of the advantages of taking action is that it stops others from nagging you.

Acceptance and Taking Action

Before you can take action in the present, you have to accept what you didn't do in the past. You may not want to pay an overdue parking ticket because you cannot accept that you should have paid it earlier. Past avoidance leads to more avoidance. Acceptance is simply acknowledging what was, what is, and what might be.

Remember the three cognitive errors of depression: 1) the depression will go on indefinitely, 2) it will spread to your whole life, and 3) it's all your fault. The first step is to accept that, because of negative thinking, you don't want to take action. Realize that believing nothing will be of any use is a symptom of depression. Even if you don't want to do what needs to be done, there is another part of you that does want to take action. Tension seeks resolution. Simply by accepting this paradox, you begin to allow it to resolve itself. Throughout your life you have done many things you have not wanted to do, but only because another part of you realized it was in your best interest to do so.

You want to avoid action because you feel locked into a bad situation or locked out of a good situation. Accept this as how you feel right now and take action anyway. If the accepted feelings are just feelings, they have no power over you. Most of the world's work is done by people who don't feel well. By accepting whatever thoughts or feelings come to you, you become free to take action in the moment.

Choice and Taking Action

When you're depressed, you rebel against being told what to do, even if you're the one giving the orders. Everyone wants to be asked, not coerced. When you try to force yourself to take action, you will encounter strong internal resistance. Imperatives of what you must do takes the fun out of any experience. You may enjoy reading, but if you think you need to read something, you don't want to.

True Needs vs. False Needs

False personal needs can never be satisfied. They are what you personally think you need to be happy and secure. You can never get enough of something you think you need, but don't really need. False need comes from the assumption that something is missing or wrong with you. True needs are the impersonal requirements to bring about something. To earn a college degree means you need to take classes and exams. Whenever you choose to have something, real needs will appear in the equation. What you want comes first and what is needed follows.

Notice the difference between telling yourself, "I need to take action," versus telling yourself, "I want to take action."

You don't want to do what you think you need to do because of the absence of choice. You're more likely to remember to get gas for the car if you tell yourself, "The car needs gas," then if you tell yourself, "I need to get gas." What makes the difference is that you take action because you choose to, rather than because you have coerced yourself.

Paradoxes

Depression is full of paradoxes. You want to get better, and at the same time, another side of you doesn't want to. You are overwhelmed, but under-act. Reality is paradox-free; the paradoxes come only from your thinking. By taking action, you're able to bypass the thinking that keeps you stuck in the paradox. After you have accepted *what is* and chosen what you would want to happen, take action quickly on what needs to be done in the moment to fulfill the want.

Graded Tasks

You can use the activity schedule to add structure to your life. Break down big projects into smaller ones, then schedule these small steps. You can see each as an experiment—a way to test whether or not you can do it.

For example, if you've been avoiding writing letters, you can schedule a period of time just to get the addresses and other materials out. Then schedule another small step, such as writing the easiest letter, adding small step after small step, all the way up to the most difficult letters. Studies find that, when people are depressed, their success experiences lead to increased motivation. So what you want to do is build in small steps that will increase your success rate, thereby increasing your motivation. Go from simple tasks to more complex ones.

This week, you can use the activity schedule to take on a task or tasks you have been avoiding, such as doing your taxes or starting to get in shape.

Tips for Taking Action

1. **Make a stand**. When you're depressed, you often fail to keep your agreements and often have major projects or commitments that you avoid. The best way to gain your own approval and raise your self-esteem is to confront these avoided tasks and projects. Take a stand for what you care about by making an active decision in favor of something you really want.

2. **Surprise yourself**. Do something that surprises you. Maybe it would surprise you to actually ask someone for a date, or to go into business for yourself, or to cut your hair off. Surprise yourself in big and small ways.

3. **Surprise someone else**. If your neighbor always drives because you're afraid of getting lost, tell your neighbor that you will drive. Take someone you don't know well out to lunch. Do something that will catch someone else by surprise.

4. **Do the easiest step**. Think of something that you have been avoiding and use it as a target for the next week. If you think that the task is too much for you, break the task down into small steps and do them one by one, easiest first. If going to the doctor is too much for you, then do the easiest step first. Look up the doctor's phone number and then write it down. Do the easiest step and you will usually start to create some momentum that will help you move on to the next step.

5. **Do the hardest step first**. Avoidance comes from your passive side. If you think you have to solve the Big Problem perfectly, you may feel overwhelmed and stalled. Try taking the opposite tack. Drop the importance of the task and simply focus on the next step in front of you, letting results unfold on their own. Look around you and pick the hardest step. If your house seems to be closing in on you and you can't seem to escape the clutter, decide to get up and clean out the biggest closet in the house. When you do the hardest step first, you create successes and build instant momentum.

6. **Do something you've never done before**. Try a different hairstyle. Explore a part of town you've never traveled in. Novelty creates curiosity and keeps you from getting stagnant. The decision to do something new starts you moving.

7. **Vary your daily schedule**. A low mood is your signal that you need to get movement into your life. Pick a project, big or small, and *do* it. You'll find

that just taking the first step of picking one will help you move. If you always get up at 8:15, get up at 7:30 instead. Watch a different TV show or decide to read instead. Do something different in your schedules and you will find you're clearer and more free. You're thinking will take you outside of yourself and you will be moving.

8. **Do the opposite of what you feel like doing.** If you feel like withdrawing from a confrontation, approach the person instead of hiding. Impulsively do the opposite of what your passive side is telling you to do and you will find that you have begun a movement away from passivity.

9. **Do a little before avoiding.** Catch yourself avoiding and then avoid your avoidance, at least for a minute or two. For example, if you've been avoiding filling out forms and decide to make yourself a cup of tea before you get started, do a little on the reports before you make the tea. You'll find that once you get started, you'll want to continue to do it. If you are still forcing yourself after a couple of minutes, stop and do your avoidance strategy and then reapply the "do a little first" strategy. Whenever you decide to put off working on a project (even for a moment), instead, do at least a small bit. After you take this small action, give your depressed side permission to leave the task to do the avoidance behavior. Then, repeat the action procedure after you've enjoyed the permitted avoidance.

10. **Choose actions that absorb your interest and concentration.** Keep it simple. Taking action can be as simple as walking across the room or putting something away. Keep your interest outside of yourself. You are at your best when your thinking, feelings, and actions are in movement toward something you want—eating, cleaning closets, taking walks, filing, making phone calls, writing letters, or grocery shopping. Passive activities, such as watching television, often are too weak to hold your interest.

11. **Aim for balance in your life.** Schedule action related to your normal activities—getting up in the morning, making breakfast, exercising, taking a walk, talking to someone, answering mail, checking the answering machine. The last activity you schedule for the day should be to sit down to schedule the next day's activities.

12. **Choose ten action steps that you do each day.** Look for what you would like to do every day, such as taking a walk or reading the paper. As you take action, focus your thinking as much as possible on what you are doing.

13. **Each night, write down ten success experiences.** You might be bogged down in the middle of the journey. You may feel that you are farther from the end than when you started. If you list your success stories, you'll find that you are closer to what you want and you'll feel better. These successes are anything you wanted to do—and did do. They can be anything as simple as getting dressed or as difficult as confronting a major problem.

14. **Act "as if."** To feel better, act "as if" you are already in this state of mind. For example, when you start to act friendly toward others, you start to feel

friendly. Although this seems to be pretending, you are acting the way you most honestly would like to feel. Ask yourself, "What action can I take that is in my best interest?" Ignore the urge to "cut off your nose to spite your face." Keep your thinking on your own best interest, and act as if you are in your active self.

15. **Plan your day**. To move out of and stay out of the reactive, passive self, you may have to repeatedly shift your thinking away from yourself and on to the project. You can benefit from planning your actions in detail if you find yourself chronically in your reactive self. Your schedule gives you a sense of direction and mastery as you focus your thinking on planned activities. Schedule one part at a time. The idea is to engage in activities, not to perform them perfectly. The benefit comes from getting involved in the actual doing.

16. **Break down big tasks**. Do one step at a time. You build self-confidence through small steps. By forcing yourself to take on too much, you sabotage your attempts to do it. Once you've taken small steps, you are ready for the next.

Homework

Homework for session 4 is as follows:

1. Pick a task you have been avoiding that you want to work on.

2. Break it down into steps, then do them.

3. For each day you want to work on the task, fill out the tasks you want to accomplish on this week's action schedule.

Action Schedule

Note: Grade activities M for Mastery and P for Pleasure

	Monday	Tuesday	Wednesday	Thursday	Friday	Saturday	Sunday
9–10							
10–11							
11–12							
12–1							
1–2							
2–3							
3–4							
4–5							
5–6							
6–7							
7–8							
8–12							

Depression Questionnaire

Choose a number from the scale below to show how much you are troubled by each problem listed. Write the number in the blank.

0	1	2	3	4	5	6	7	8
Hardly at all		Slightly troublesome		Definitely troublesome		Markedly troublesome		Very severely troublesome

_____ 1. Feeling miserable, empty, or depressed

_____ 2. Feeling bad about yourself

_____ 3. Feeling discouraged or hopeless about the future

_____ 4. Automatic negative thoughts coming into your mind

_____ 5. Feeling bad or discouraged about your life

_____ 6. Other feelings (describe) _____

_____ 7. How would you rate the present state of your depression symptoms on the scale below? Please circle one number between 0 and 8.

0	1	2	3	4	5	6	7	8
No symptoms present		Slightly disturbing/ not really disturbing		Definitely disturbing/ disabling		Markedly disturbing/ disabling		Very severely disturbing/ disabling

Weekly Practice Record

Goals for Week: Date:

1.

2.

3.

MON	TUES	WED	THUR	FRI	SAT	SUN

Session 5

Mastering Feeling Symptoms

How You Think and Feel

Once you've begun to work on some of your behavioral symptoms with the action schedule, the second cluster of depression symptoms you want to focus on are your feelings. The negative feelings of depression come from your thoughts. How you *think*—about yourself and your experiences—is the single most important factor in how you feel. When you see yourself as a loser and the world as a hostile, unfriendly place, you will naturally feel bad. The feelings are doing their job, you are just feeding yourself skewed data. Negative conclusions about yourself and about your world keep you from feeling good.

When you're depressed, you distort your experiences to fit your negative thinking. Positive experiences that normally would undercut this negative view are ignored or distorted. Your negativity warps your perceptions and you begin to make systematic errors in your thinking. This isn't something you voluntarily choose to do; rather, it's the very essence of depression.

When you become depressed, you conclude that you can't help but lose. This in turn generates a stream of negative thoughts that lead to bad feelings. For example, if you think other people don't like you (whether or not this is true makes no difference), you'll feel sad because you believe you've lost their approval. If you believe tasks you normally do are too tough, you'll feel hopeless. If you think people will put you down or criticize you, you'll feel anxious and start withdrawing from people. If you think you can't make the right decisions no matter what, you'll feel insecure.

Your bad feelings keep this process going. For example, negative feelings, such as sadness, stimulate more negative thoughts of yourself and your world, which lead to more negative feelings. When you feel hopeless, you'll use your lack of accomplishments as further proof that there is no hope. You're caught in a vicious cycle. You have negative thoughts that cause bad feelings, which in turn cause more negative thoughts. This process keeps your depression going. While it's difficult to directly change your feelings, you can, with practice, learn how to choose different thoughts. By systematically thinking differently, you can avoid future depressions.

The Emotions of Depression

In one sense, your bad feelings are the most prominent cluster of depression. Feeling chronically unhappy is one of the first signs that you're starting to get depressed. You feel sad and blue throughout the day. Sadness by itself is not depression. You can feel sad without being depressed. Sadness can be appropriate and useful to you. For example, when someone dies, you feel appropriately sad so you can accept this loss. However, the sadness in depression isn't helpful.

Guilt can be another feeling symptom of depression. When you're depressed, you often believe you've let people down or that you've done some other terrible act and that means you're a bad person.

Loneliness is a common symptom of depression. You might feel cut off and isolated from others and think you've lost the ability to relate to others. Anxiety often accompanies depression. You might experience fear and dread much of the time.

Finally, many people experience exaggerated shame as an emotional symptom of depression. You may be ashamed of being depressed—ashamed to seek help or ashamed over the event that preceded the depression, such as divorce or loss of a job.

Using the Thought Record

The second major tool of this program is the thought record. You'll find one completed thought record and blank copies for you to complete at the end of this chapter. Because thinking, ideas, and beliefs lead to the symptoms of depression, you can use the thought record as a systematic way to become aware of and change your thoughts. The thought record is a tool to help you consider a situation that makes you feel bad, and then discover which thoughts prompted your negative feelings. Once you have an awareness of these damaging and distorted thoughts, you can begin to challenge them, undermining the power they have to keep you depressed.

Reflect on the thoughts that came up when you used the activity schedule. Did any thoughts try to prevent you from doing the exercise? Did these thoughts actually stop you from doing the exercise, or were you able to challenge them and do the exercise anyway? Common negative thoughts that arise for depressed people when forced with trying something new are thoughts like "This is stupid"; "It won't help me"; "I don't want to do it now"; ""I'll do it later"; "I can't remember what I did"; "It's too much work"; "It's too hard."

Thoughts like these keep you stuck in depression. They stop you from initiating activity that can get you to overcome your depression, and because you've discontinued the activity, they stop you from getting satisfaction from activities.

Cognitive Distortions

As your therapist discussed before, when you're depressed, you make three cognitive distortions: 1) you *jump to conclusions* and believe negative situation will go on forever in the future ("Because he didn't call, he never will"); 2) you *overgeneralize* from the specific loss or disappointment to all areas of your life ("I can't do anything"; "Everything bad always happens to me"); 3) you see the loss as due to an inherent fault and think in *either/or terms* ("Either I'm beautiful or I'm ugly"; "Either I'm accepted or I'm rejected").

Although distorted, the thoughts seem plausible to you and the more depressed you become, the more you believe them. A vicious cycle starts—the thoughts create the symptoms and the symptoms create more thoughts.

To undercut your depression, you'll need to challenge the thoughts that are creating the symptoms. Like a scientist, you want to examine your thoughts to see if they're true. You can use the thought record to make this easier and more systematic. Take a look at one of the blank thought records at the end of this session to see how they work.

As you can see, in the first column of the thought record is the situation that came before the symptom. This could be an actual event leading to an unpleasant emotion (a friend criticizes you) or it could be a stream of thoughts, daydreams, or recollections leading to an unpleasant emotion (you start to think about how you acted at a party). You want to become aware of these situations because awareness is the first step. The quicker you recognize the situation, the quicker you can choose new thoughts.

The next column is for your subjective experience or the symptom of depression. This may be an emotion, such as guilt, anxiety, or sadness. It may be a behavior—avoiding a situation, for example. It could be difficulty in making a decision or a problem concentrating.

Next to each symptom, you will rate its severity from 1 to 10. If you were experiencing moderate sadness, for example, you might rate your symptom as 4. For severe sadness, you might rate it as 9. If you have trouble recognizing the symptoms of your depression, it may take you a while just to become tuned into what your specific symptoms are.

In the third column you'll write the automatic thoughts and beliefs that cause the symptoms. For example, you will feel guilty if you have thoughts such as, "I've done something terrible that I shouldn't have done." You'll feel anxious if you think there's some danger lurking in the future; sad if you feel you've lost something.

You may have a thought that encourages you to get out of a situation ("I can't stand it here, I have to leave"). The thoughts may be ones that are blocking you from trying some new activity, thoughts like "I'm not interested, I don't want to do that." Perhaps you don't have a specific thought, but the event has some underlying meaning to you, such as "Failing the test means I can't do anything right."

Your therapist will help you practice using the thought record. Think back over the last day or two to a situation where you had some negative feelings—sad, anxious, or guilty. Write out the situation on the thought record and what the emotions were, rating the intensity of the emotion from 1 to 10. Then, by re-experiencing this in your imagination, catch the thought that came with it, the negative thought you had about the situation. Write the thought (or thoughts) in the appropriate column. Finally, see if you can spot the distortions in your thinking and write them down. Perhaps it was 1) jumping to conclusions about your future; 2) overgeneralizing about your life; or 3) either/or thinking about yourself.

Homework

Homework for session 5 is as follows:

1. Fill out at least one thought record a day.

2. Write: a) the situation, b) the thought, and c) the type of error (jumping to conclusions, overgeneralization, or either/or thinking).

3. Use an instant replay technique. If you have some negative feelings and can't quite catch the thoughts, replay the feelings over and over until you can. Look for the *meaning* of the situation. Ask yourself, "What is the significance of the situation to me? What are the consequences?"

Thought Record

Situation	Feeling	Automatic Thoughts	Thinking Error
What were you doing or thinking when you started to feel bad?	What symptom did you notice (e.g., anger, apathy)? How bad did you feel (1-10, 10 being worst)?	What was going through your mind immediately before you felt bad?	#1—jumping to conclusions about the future; #2—overgeneralizing about your life; #3—either/or thinking about yourself.
At work	Sad	My life is over. I have nothing to look forward to.	#1
Thinking about my marriage	Hurt, angry	It's all my fault. Nothing will work out.	#3 and #2

Thought Record

Situation	Feeling	Automatic Thoughts	Thinking Error
What were you doing or thinking when you started to feel bad?	What symptom did you notice (e.g., anger, apathy)? How bad did you feel (1-10, 10 being worst)?	What was going through your mind immediately before you felt bad?	#1—jumping to conclusions about the future; #2—overgeneralizing about your life; #3—either/or thinking about yourself.

Thought Record

Situation	Feeling	Automatic Thoughts	Thinking Error
What were you doing or thinking when you started to feel bad?	What symptom did you notice (e.g., anger, apathy)? How bad did you feel (1-10, 10 being worst)?	What was going through your mind immediately before you felt bad?	#1—jumping to conclusions about the future; #2—overgeneralizing about your life; #3—either/or thinking about yourself.

Thought Record

Situation	Feeling	Automatic Thoughts	Thinking Error
What were you doing or thinking when you started to feel bad?	What symptom did you notice (e.g., anger, apathy)? How bad did you feel (1-10, 10 being worst)?	What was going through your mind immediately before you felt bad?	#1—jumping to conclusions about the future; #2—overgeneralizing about your life; #3—either/or thinking about yourself.

Thought Record

Situation	Feeling	Automatic Thoughts	Thinking Error
What were you doing or thinking when you started to feel bad?	What symptom did you notice (e.g., anger, apathy)? How bad did you feel (1-10, 10 being worst)?	What was going through your mind immediately before you felt bad?	#1—jumping to conclusions about the future; #2—overgeneralizing about your life; #3—either/or thinking about yourself.

Thought Record

Situation	Feeling	Automatic Thoughts	Thinking Error
What were you doing or thinking when you started to feel bad?	What symptom did you notice (e.g., anger, apathy)? How bad did you feel (1-10, 10 being worst)?	What was going through your mind immediately before you felt bad?	#1—jumping to conclusions about the future; #2—overgeneralizing about your life; #3—either/or thinking about yourself.

Thought Record

Situation	Feeling	Automatic Thoughts	Thinking Error
What were you doing or thinking when you started to feel bad?	What symptom did you notice (e.g., anger, apathy)? How bad did you feel (1-10, 10 being worst)?	What was going through your mind immediately before you felt bad?	#1—jumping to conclusions about the future; #2—overgeneralizing about your life; #3—either/or thinking about yourself.

Thought Record

Situation	Feeling	Automatic Thoughts	Thinking Error
What were you doing or thinking when you started to feel bad?	What symptom did you notice (e.g., anger, apathy)? How bad did you feel (1-10, 10 being worst)?	What was going through your mind immediately before you felt bad?	#1—jumping to conclusions about the future; #2—overgeneralizing about your life; #3—either/or thinking about yourself.

Thought Record

Situation	Feeling	Automatic Thoughts	Thinking Error
What were you doing or thinking when you started to feel bad?	What symptom did you notice (e.g., anger, apathy)? How bad did you feel (1-10, 10 being worst)?	What was going through your mind immediately before you felt bad?	#1—jumping to conclusions about the future; #2—overgeneralizing about your life; #3—either/or thinking about yourself.

Thought Record

Situation	Feeling	Automatic Thoughts	Thinking Error
What were you doing or thinking when you started to feel bad?	What symptom did you notice (e.g., anger, apathy)? How bad did you feel (1-10, 10 being worst)?	What was going through your mind immediately before you felt bad?	#1—jumping to conclusions about the future; #2—overgeneralizing about your life; #3—either/or thinking about yourself.

Thought Record

Situation	Feeling	Automatic Thoughts	Thinking Error
What were you doing or thinking when you started to feel bad?	What symptom did you notice (e.g., anger, apathy)? How bad did you feel (1-10, 10 being worst)?	What was going through your mind immediately before you felt bad?	#1—jumping to conclusions about the future; #2—overgeneralizing about your life; #3—either/or thinking about yourself.

Action Schedule

Note: Grade activities M for Mastery and P for Pleasure

	Monday	Tuesday	Wednesday	Thursday	Friday	Saturday	Sunday
9–10							
10–11							
11–12							
12–1							
1–2							
2–3							
3–4							
4–5							
5–6							
6–7							
7–8							
8–12							

Depression Questionnaire

Choose a number from the scale below to show how much you are troubled by each problem listed. Write the number in the blank.

0	1	2	3	4	5	6	7	8
Hardly at all		Slightly troublesome		Definitely troublesome		Markedly troublesome		Very severely troublesome

_____ 1. Feeling miserable, empty, or depressed

_____ 2. Feeling bad about yourself

_____ 3. Feeling discouraged or hopeless about the future

_____ 4. Automatic negative thoughts coming into your mind

_____ 5. Feeling bad or discouraged about your life

_____ 6. Other feelings (describe) _____

_____ 7. How would you rate the present state of your depression symptoms on the scale below? Please circle one number between 0 and 8.

0	1	2	3	4	5	6	7	8
No symptoms present		Slightly disturbing/ not really disturbing		Definitely disturbing/ disabling		Markedly disturbing/ disabling		Very severely disturbing/ disabling

Weekly Practice Record

Goals for Week: Date:

1.

2.

3.

MON	TUES	WED	THUR	FRI	SAT	SUN

Center for Epidemiologic Studies Depressed Mood Scale (CES-D)

Using the scale below, indicate the number which best describes how often you felt, or behaved this way DURING THE PAST WEEK.

0 = Rarely or none of the time (less than 1 time)

1 = Some or a little of the time (1-2 days)

2 = Occasionally or a moderate amount of time (3-4 days)

3 = Most or all of the time (5-7 days)

DURING THE PAST WEEK

_____ 1. I was bothered by things that usually don't bother me.

_____ 2. I did not feel like eating; my appetite was poor.

_____ 3. I felt that I could not shake off the blues even with help from my family or friends.

_____ 4. I felt that I was just as good as other people.

_____ 5. I had trouble keeping my mind on what I was doing.

_____ 6. I felt depressed.

_____ 7. I felt that everything I did was an effort.

_____ 8. I felt hopeful about the future.

_____ 9. I thought my life had been a failure.

_____ 10. I felt fearful.

_____ 11. My sleep was restless.

_____ 12. I was happy.

_____ 13. I talked less than usual.

_____ 14. I felt lonely.

_____ 15. People were unfriendly.

_____ 16. I enjoyed life.

_____ 17. I had crying spells.

_____ 18. I felt sad.

_____ 19. I felt that people dislike me.

_____ 20. I could not get "going."

Session 6

Challenging Negative Thoughts

Honing Your Thought Record Skills

What kind of problems did you have in filling out the thought record? Did you have trouble thinking of a situation? Once you realize that you can choose to think differently, you'll begin to look for these situations and welcome them as a chance to learn new skills.

You can use your own body's reactions as cues to let you know when you reach a situation that you'll want to use the thought record on. Often, the symptoms of depression have some effect on your body. Tight muscles often indicate unpleasant emotions. Those times you tend to want to avoid situations and people are also times to look for thoughts to do a thought record on.

Did you have problems recognizing what emotion you had? Many people aren't used to labeling their emotions. Sometimes you have to work backwards—going from thought to emotion. Thoughts about loss, for example, imply sadness. If you have thoughts about some danger coming up in the future, this leads to anxiety. Anger is feeling like people are taking unfair advantage of you and you need to get even. Guilt usually comes up over breaking some moral code. Shame is from the fear that people will find out that you've broken some moral or social code.

Did you have trouble rating the severity of the symptom? Remember, your rating is completely subjective. There is no right or wrong answer—only your best guess.

Did you have difficulty recognizing and catching your automatic thoughts? Because this skill is new to you, it may take some practice before you're able to determine exactly what your thinking is. Not because this is buried deep in your unconscious, or because you don't recognize it, but because you aren't trained to tune into your thinking. One strategy that's helpful is to slowly replay the situation in your mind—as though you were watching a movie. By doing this, you can be more aware of what you're thinking.

Often your automatic thoughts are fragmented and just barely out of your ordinary awareness, so you have to look intensely for them. Sometimes you have to simply keep writing your thoughts down until you get to the ones that are causing the problem. You start with the most obvious thoughts and go to the ones that you're less aware of.

One way to get at these thoughts is to ask yourself for the meaning. "What does this mean to me as a person? What do the consequences of the event mean to me? What does it mean about my future or about the type of world I live in?" Don't forget that sometimes you think in visual images instead of in words. In these cases, write down the image you had.

The last step of the homework assignment was to examine your thoughts to see whether or not they contained one of the three cognitive distortions: 1) jumping to conclusions, 2) overgeneralizing, and 3) either/or thinking. The next step is to generate answers, or new ways of thinking. One of the best ways to examine your thoughts is through careful questioning of them, and through this examination new, more productive thoughts will emerge. You can use three questions to examine your automatic thoughts. These questions can become answers in themselves, or they can produce answers that allow you to see the untruths and distortions in your automatic thoughts.

The three most important questions are:

1. **What's the evidence that the thought is true?** For example, the thought, "I'm a complete failure because my children don't love me, so I can never be happy," should be looked at objectively. What is the evidence for and against?

2. **What's another way of looking at it?** For example, inattention from children can be looked at as evidence that either "They don't love me" or "They're busy with their own lives."

3. **Even if it is true, how bad are the consequences?** For example, you may see that "Even if they don't love me, I can still choose to be happy." Typically, when you're depressed, you use thoughts like, "My children don't love me" as evidence that "I'm no good, I don't deserve their love" and beyond that, "I don't deserve anything."

Use these questions to generate answers to your depression-generated thoughts.

For example, suppose you feel bad because you believe people don't like you. The first question to ask about that belief is, "What's the evidence?" Your answer might be, "Not everyone dislikes me"; "It's just a few people"; "I'm taking this out of context." The second question is, "What's another way of looking at this?" You might realize that there will always be a certain number of people who will dislike you and that this should be expected. Most people are so concerned with their own interests that they don't have enough time to spend worrying about you.

The third question is "So what?" It's helpful to take your ideas to their ultimate conclusion, assuming your perceptions are correct and see what the result would be. In this case, you might think, "Even if everyone disliked me, I wouldn't need to be depressed. I would find out why I'm not liked so I could change if I wanted to, but I don't have to be depressed about it." Your action could be to check out perceptions as to whether or not people like you.

Put these answers in the column under "Answers." Then write down what action you can take to deal constructively with the problem or action that will make you feel better.

As the last step, see if there was any change in your emotional reactions after you take the action. Write down your new rating of emotional reaction. See the example in your manual.

You can learn to lessen your negative feelings by correcting your erroneous thinking. Remember, bad feelings are maintained by thoughts that precede them. Often, these thoughts are fleeting and occur automatically, so that you are not even aware of them. You can see examples of typical thinking errors and ways to correct them in table 1.

In addition to answering your negative and distorted thoughts, you'll need to act on the new, more realistic thoughts you develop as alternatives. By acting on new thoughts, you not only come to believe them intellectually, but emotionally as well. Table 2 provides some ways that you can act on your new thoughts. Whenever possible, directly test your beliefs against reality.

Homework

Homework for session 6 is as follows:

> 1. Completely fill out at least one extended thought record each day, making sure to use the three questions reviewed in this session: What's the evidence? What's an alternative view? So what if is is true?

Table 1

Three Typical Thinking Errors Associated with Depression and "Rational Answers"

Type of Error	Examples	Rational Answer
Error # 1: Jumping to conclusions about the future.	**Taking events out of context:** After a social error, focusing on one or two comments; "I completely blew it, everyone will think I'm a fool."	"I may have said one or two inappropriate things, but all in all, it was a good meeting."
	Catastrophizing: "I have a swollen gland, it must be cancer. My life is over."	"There's no evidence. I'll just have to check it out."
	Magical thinking: "I'll be punished forever because of my past bad deeds."	"There's no rational reason to believe this. This is only a reflection of my depressive thinking."
Error # 2: Overgeneralizing about your life.	**Dramatizing:** "I always fail. I fail at everything I ever try."	That's not true. Actually, I succeed at most of what I try."
	Magnifying: Blowing negative events out of proportion; "This is the worst thing that could happen to me."	"What happened is just a fact. I upset myself by making it so important. There are much worse things that could happen to me."
	Minimizing: Glossing over the saving and positive factors; "I'm ruined, I have nothing left and will wind up being put out in the street."	"I'm not completely at the end. I have friends and resources."
Error #3: Either/or thinking about self	**Not taking into account the full continuum:** "Either I'm a winner or a loser."	"This is black and white thinking and it doesn't take into account the grays. I'm actually about average in most areas."
	Comparing and judging unfairly: Comparing self with someone else and ignoring the basic differences; "They have everything, I have nothing."	"I am who I am. Everyone is different, so these are false comparisons."
	Self-blame: Blaming total self rather than specific behaviors that can be changed; "I'm just no good. I don't finish anything."	"I do have a problem with procrastination. I'll just have to work on it."
	Personalizing: Thinking all situations and events revolve around you; "Everyone was looking at me and wondering why I was there."	"I'm not the center of the world. Most people are too concerned about themselves to think about me. Because I feel something is true doesn't mean that it is."

Table 2
The Role of Action in Altering Thinking

Distorted Thoughts	Answers	Action
"I can't do anything about my depression."	"If I try, I can beat it. I can learn something new."	Write out answers to negative thoughts.
"I don't enjoy anything."	"Maybe if I do something I used to do, I'll have fun."	Go to a movie.
"It's too hard for me to do housework."	"I'll try an experiment and work on it for 10 minutes."	Work on it for 10 minutes.
"I bet this lump is cancer."	"I better see a doctor to check it out."	See doctor.
"I'm ashamed of how old and ugly I look."	"Shame is self-created. If I don't think it's shameful, I won't feel like it is."	Go out in public.
"If I disagree with my sister, she'll dislike me."	"I have survived quite well the disappointment of others before."	Express your disagreement to your sister.
"I made a terrible mistake in hiring an incompetent carpenter. What if people find out?"	"It's a mistake to think I can never make a mistake. So what if they find out? It won't be the end of the world."	Tell someone about the mistake.

Extended Thought Record

Situation	Feeling	Thoughts	Error	Answers	Action to Take	Outcome
What were you doing or thinking?	What were you feeling? 1-10	What went through your mind?	#1 jump to conclusions; #2 over-generalize; #3 either/or	What's the evidence? What's an alternative explanation? So what?	How can you test this out or improve the situation?	How do you feel now?
2/8 Driving in car, thinking	Guilty #9	I ruined my life.	#1 and #2	There is no evidence. I just feel this way because I'm depressed.	Talk to others about it	Guilty #3
2/9 Home thinking about depression	Anxious #8	What if I never get out of this? I'm cursed.	#1 and #2	All the evidence indicates I will get over it. So what if I don't. I can still live my life.	Clean kitchen	Anxious #2

Extended Thought Record

Situation	Feeling	Thoughts	Error	Answers	Action to Take	Outcome
What were you doing or thinking?	What were you feeling? 1-10	What went through your mind?	#1 jump to conclusions; #2 over-generalize; #3 either/or	What's the evidence? What's an alternative explanation? So what?	How can you test this out or improve the situation?	How do you feel now?

Extended Thought Record

Situation	Feeling	Thoughts	Error	Answers	Action to Take	Outcome
What were you doing or thinking?	What were you feeling? 1-10	What went through your mind?	#1 jump to conclusions; #2 over-generalize; #3 either/or	What's the evidence? What's an alternative explanation? So what?	How can you test this out or improve the situation?	How do you feel now?

Extended Thought Record

Situation	Feeling	Thoughts	Error	Answers	Action to Take	Outcome
What were you doing or thinking?	What were you feeling? 1-10	What went through your mind?	#1 jump to conclusions; #2 over-generalize; #3 either/or	What's the evidence? What's an alternative explanation? So what?	How can you test this out or improve the situation?	How do you feel now?

Extended Thought Record

Situation	Feeling	Thoughts	Error	Answers	Action to Take	Outcome
What were you doing or thinking?	What were you feeling? 1-10	What went through your mind?	#1 jump to conclusions; #2 over-generalize; #3 either/or	What's the evidence? What's an alternative explanation? So what?	How can you test this out or improve the situation?	How do you feel now?

Extended Thought Record

Situation	Feeling	Thoughts	Error	Answers	Action to Take	Outcome
What were you doing or thinking?	What were you feeling? 1-10	What went through your mind?	#1 jump to conclusions; #2 over-generalize; #3 either/or	What's the evidence? What's an alternative explanation? So what?	How can you test this out or improve the situation?	How do you feel now?

Extended Thought Record

Situation	Feeling	Thoughts	Error	Answers	Action to Take	Outcome
What were you doing or thinking?	What were you feeling? 1-10	What went through your mind?	#1 jump to conclusions; #2 over-generalize; #3 either/or	What's the evidence? What's an alternative explanation? So what?	How can you test this out or improve the situation?	How do you feel now?

Extended Thought Record

Situation	Feeling	Thoughts	Error	Answers	Action to Take	Outcome
What were you doing or thinking?	What were you feeling? 1-10	What went through your mind?	#1 jump to conclusions; #2 over-generalize; #3 either/or	What's the evidence? What's an alternative explanation? So what?	How can you test this out or improve the situation?	How do you feel now?

Extended Thought Record

Situation	Feeling	Thoughts	Error	Answers	Action to Take	Outcome
What were you doing or thinking?	What were you feeling? 1-10	What went through your mind?	#1 jump to conclusions; #2 over-generalize; #3 either/or	What's the evidence? What's an alternative explanation? So what?	How can you test this out or improve the situation?	How do you feel now?

Extended Thought Record

Situation	Feeling	Thoughts	Error	Answers	Action to Take	Outcome
What were you doing or thinking?	What were you feeling? 1-10	What went through your mind?	#1 jump to conclusions; #2 over-generalize; #3 either/or	What's the evidence? What's an alternative explanation? So what?	How can you test this out or improve the situation?	How do you feel now?

Extended Thought Record

Situation	Feeling	Thoughts	Error	Answers	Action to Take	Outcome
What were you doing or thinking?	What were you feeling? 1-10	What went through your mind?	#1 jump to conclusions; #2 over-generalize; #3 either/or	What's the evidence? What's an alternative explanation? So what?	How can you test this out or improve the situation?	How do you feel now?

Action Schedule

Note: Grade activities M for Mastery and P for Pleasure

	Monday	Tuesday	Wednesday	Thursday	Friday	Saturday	Sunday
9–10							
10–11							
11–12							
12–1							
1–2							
2–3							
3–4							
4–5							
5–6							
6–7							
7–8							
8–12							

Depression Questionnaire

Choose a number from the scale below to show how much you are troubled by each problem listed. Write the number in the blank.

0	1	2	3	4	5	6	7	8
Hardly at all		Slightly troublesome		Definitely troublesome		Markedly troublesome		Very severely troublesome

_____ 1. Feeling miserable, empty, or depressed

_____ 2. Feeling bad about yourself

_____ 3. Feeling discouraged or hopeless about the future

_____ 4. Automatic negative thoughts coming into your mind

_____ 5. Feeling bad or discouraged about your life

_____ 6. Other feelings (describe) _____

_____ 7. How would you rate the present state of your depression symptoms on the scale below? Please circle one number between 0 and 8.

0	1	2	3	4	5	6	7	8
No symptoms present		Slightly disturbing/ not really disturbing		Definitely disturbing/ disabling		Markedly disturbing/ disabling		Very severely disturbing/ disabling

Weekly Practice Record

Goals for Week: Date:

1.

2.

3.

MON	TUES	WED	THUR	FRI	SAT	SUN

Session 7

Dropping Thoughts

Tips for Using Your Thought Records

Did you have any problems with the thought record this week? Were you able to find alternative explanations that more closely reflect reality? Were you able to see any errors in your thinking, such as overgeneralizations? Did you find more useful, adaptive ways of looking at the situation that troubled you? In the final column, did you re-rate the symptoms? Did you feel less guilt, anxiety, sadness?

Remember why you're doing the thought record. You aren't doing it just to see that you make mistakes in thinking, but also to get some symptom relief—to feel better and to act in a more adaptable, productive manner. That's the ultimate purpose of doing the thought record.

Using the thought record effectively is a skill that takes time to develop. You'll get better and better at it, finding it easier to do as you go along.

When you're depressed, you'll have strong urges not to fill the record out—mainly because you don't want to focus on something that's unpleasant. In fact, you may often initially feel worse when you start to complete the form. However, if you can stick it out and make it through the form, you'll eventually feel better. But you have to actually fill it out to get any benefit from it.

Having to sit down and write about your thoughts and feelings may feel burdensome to you. You may wonder why you can't just work it out in your mind. Writing the material out is crucial because what you're working on is just too difficult to work out in your head. Writing it all down and reflecting on your thoughts is largely why this form of therapy works: it pushes you to take the time, space, and opportunity necessary to gain a real awareness of the thoughts and beliefs that have been controlling your feelings.

You can expect that it'll take some time for you to become really comfortable using the thought record. You'll have to do at least twenty-five forms before you master it, which is why there are so many blank copies of it in your manual. You're encouraged to complete a thought record any time an incident brings on bad feelings. The more thought records you can complete, the easier they will become—and the better you'll feel.

First, you have to become aware of your symptoms and the thoughts behind them. Second, you have to answer these thoughts with more realistic and adaptive thoughts. Third, you have to act on the new thoughts. It's not enough just to talk to yourself, you have to take some concrete steps.

One of the spaces on the record asks you to think up an action you can take. The action becomes a sort of experiment in which you can test your beliefs. If you're not sure whether or not your beliefs are true, this action is a way for you to go out and check them out. You may want to call someone up and be more assertive just to see if you will, in fact, be rejected. You may want to approach a person or place you've been avoiding and actually see if you really do botch it, as your thoughts tell you. You may just want to write down the next time this type of situation reappears, using an experience that happened by chance as a sort of experiment.

Thinking: The Third Symptom Cluster

The third symptom cluster of depression involves how you think. While your thinking is behind your other symptoms, the symptoms in this cluster revolve around your general thinking ability. If you're depressed, you might have trouble concentrating. You probably have a hard time keeping your mind on what you're doing.

Another of the thinking symptoms of depression is memory problems. You may forget the names of people you've known for years, or forget something as familiar as your address. If you're taking a class, you may have trouble retaining the material. This is not a permanent memory loss; it's only the result of your mind being so crowded by thoughts (many of them negative) that you lose track of everyday thoughts.

Difficulty in making decisions is another symptom in this cluster. You may be agonizing over major decisions or you may be having trouble making even minor decisions, such as where to stop for lunch or what clothes to wear. Again, this can be attributed to the overwhelming "static" of negative thinking that depressed people suffer under. And many of these thoughts undermine your confidence ("You're a failure"; "You can't do anything right"), which makes it extra difficult to trust the decisions you make.

Another thinking symptom is intrusive thoughts of wanting to harm yourself. This is usually a clear sign of depression. These symptoms come from over-thinking, under-acting and under-feeling. To lessen these symptoms, you want to get out of your thinking.

Noting and Dropping Thoughts

You often won't have a chance to write out answers to your negative thoughts. After all, when you're barraged with thoughts, you only have time and energy to write out and disprove the really powerful ones. But what about the multitude of smaller negative thoughts that pop up constantly throughout the day? Once you realize they are simply distortions, you can note and drop them in your mind ("That's a thought . . . now drop it"). You may have to do this a number of times before the thought fades away, but eventually, starved for attention, the thought will fade.

Thought noting is a powerful tool for a number of reasons. One of the most important is that by noting thoughts, you're becoming aware of them. Once you become aware of them, you can answer them and fundamentally alter the way you are looking at the world. It's a much better policy to bring thoughts out in the open by acknowledging them rather than stuff them. If you ignore them, they tend to go underground to work on you and to make you more depressed. But once they're out in the open, you can work on them in the bright light of day.

Noting your thoughts will distance you from them. This will provide you with quick relief and actually can make the thoughts decrease in number. With some distance you can see that thoughts aren't necessarily facts. You can say to yourself, "Okay, that's another thought. I don't have to believe it, just note it and let it go."

Whenever you start to feel bad, tune into what you're thinking. You're sure to find some negative thoughts knocking around in your head, dragging you down. As soon as you become aware of them, you can note and drop them. At first, their number may seem to be increasing, but this is only because you're becoming more aware of them. Be careful when you're noting negative thoughts that you don't jump to conclusions, such as, "I'm incurable because I have so many of these thoughts."

You can write down how many you have, if you choose. Some people find just counting their negative thoughts helpful. They can see that their number of thoughts varies from day to day and from situation to situation, becoming more aware of what situations or variables are more likely to produce depression-causing thoughts.

At first, you may want to begin by just noting the times you feel bad. Gradually, you'll be able to tune more and more into the specific thoughts you have. You can use thought noting for all of your symptoms of depression.

Continue Working with the Thought Record

In addition to simply noting your thoughts, you'll need to continue practicing with the thought record. It's important to *use* the thought record, not just to know about it. When you're depressed, you'll experience a natural resistance to altering your emotional state. You can combat this resistance to help you increase the chances you'll use the thought record by doing the following:

- Use any aids that you've developed to help you do what you've been putting off. One client, for example, used one of the verbal cues he'd created early in therapy to get him more active: "To cope with depression, I want to learn to think straight." He repeated it frequently to himself to remind himself to use the thought record. When another client started to feel bad, she would say to herself, "I'm talking myself into being sick." This was a cue for her to start writing down and answering her thoughts.

- If you have difficulty making yourself sit down and write out your thoughts, you can select a specific time and place in your house to work on the homework. Try setting a kitchen timer for fifteen or twenty minutes to work on your thoughts. Once you get this down to a routine, it'll increase the chances that you'll do it. If you decide to work on it at 7 P.M. each night, that's one decision fewer you'll have to make for the day.

- Another strategy is to remove distractions as you start to do a thought record. For example, if you're settling in to write your thoughts down, you may want to remove books, magazines, or anything else on the table or desk that will distract you from doing your homework.

- Some people have found that rewarding themselves for doing their thought records is helpful. For example, if you normally read the paper when you get home from work, you may want to postpone that until you've done your homework. Or, you may want to do it after dinner, using dessert as a reward.

- Others have said talking to themselves is helpful, actually having conversations in their heads. They talk to their bodies: "Arms, pick up the pencil, start writing." Sometimes saying this out loud makes it even easier to get yourself moving.

- One of the symptoms of depression is a strong wish to avoid activity. You may feel this symptom strongly when you sit down to complete your thought record. You'll be able to come up with many reasons why you don't want to do it ("It won't help"; "Why bother?" "It's too much trouble"). Remember, you can always work on the thoughts that stop you from doing homework. You can find out what the reasons are behind it and work at challenging them. For example, if you think your problems are too big to be solved, you can write out answers to this objection—"I don't know unless I give it a try, maybe my problem is that I'm making things too complicated. I should try to simplify things. Why don't I try an experiment of actually doing my thought record to see if it works?"

- You may have unrealistically high standards about the thought record. You may want to do it perfectly. Don't lose track of the main goal of the thought record, which is to help you with your symptoms, not to be completed perfectly.

- You may think that you simply don't have enough time to devote to your thought record. Here, it's a question of setting priorities on what you want to get done. Your mind, unwilling to change, will offer many things that you *must* get done before you can work on homework, but mostly these things have exaggerated importance. They're just excuses for not doing your thought records. Remember, you always have a choice in the matter.

The Benefit of Critical Incidents

When you're experiencing one of the symptoms of depression, there will be points where you'll have to make a decision about addressing your feelings. It's important to become aware of these *critical incidents*: those moments when you can decide to start working on your sadness, avoidance, or any other symptoms. Each of these incidents is like a fork in the road, an opportunity to get on the path to feeling better. A good general strategy to take advantage of these opportunities is to do the opposite of what your instincts urge. If you feel like giving up and going to bed, take constructive action instead—*approach* instead of *avoid*.

Homework

Homework for session 7 is as follows:

1. Fill out at least one extended thought record each day.

2. Practice noting and dropping thoughts.

Extended Thought Record

Situation	Feeling	Thoughts	Error	Answers	Action to Take	Outcome
What were you doing or thinking?	What were you feeling? 1-10	What went through your mind?	#1 jump to conclusions; #2 over-generalize; #3 either/or	What's the evidence? What's an alternative explanation? So what?	How can you test this out or improve the situation?	How do you feel now?

Extended Thought Record

Situation	Feeling	Thoughts	Error	Answers	Action To Take	Outcome
What were you doing or thinking?	What were you feeling? 1-10	What went through your mind?	#1 jump to conclusions #2 over-generalize #3 either/or	What's the evidence? What's an alternative explanation? So what?	How can you test this out or improve the situation?	How do you feel now?

Extended Thought Record

Situation	Feeling	Thoughts	Error	Answers	Action to Take	Outcome
What were you doing or thinking?	What were you feeling? 1-10	What went through your mind?	#1 jump to conclusions; #2 over-generalize; #3 either/or	What's the evidence? What's an alternative explanation? So what?	How can you test this out or improve the situation?	How do you feel now?

Extended Thought Record

Situation	Feeling	Thoughts	Error	Answers	Action To Take	Outcome
What were you doing or thinking?	What were you feeling? 1-10	What went through your mind?	#1 jump to conclusions #2 over-generalize #3 either/or	What's the evidence? What's an alternative explanation? So what?	How can you test this out or improve the situation?	How do you feel now?

Extended Thought Record

Situation	Feeling	Thoughts	Error	Answers	Action to Take	Outcome
What were you doing or thinking?	What were you feeling? 1-10	What went through your mind?	#1 jump to conclusions; #2 over-generalize; #3 either/or	What's the evidence? What's an alternative explanation? So what?	How can you test this out or improve the situation?	How do you feel now?

Extended Thought Record

Situation	Feeling	Thoughts	Error	Answers	Action To Take	Outcome
What were you doing or thinking?	What were you feeling? 1-10	What went through your mind?	#1 jump to conclusions #2 over-generalize #3 either/or	What's the evidence? What's an alternative explanation? So what?	How can you test this out or improve the situation?	How do you feel now?

Extended Thought Record

Situation	Feeling	Thoughts	Error	Answers	Action to Take	Outcome
What were you doing or thinking?	What were you feeling? 1-10	What went through your mind?	#1 jump to conclusions; #2 over-generalize; #3 either/or	What's the evidence? What's an alternative explanation? So what?	How can you test this out or improve the situation?	How do you feel now?

Extended Thought Record

Situation	Feeling	Thoughts	Error	Answers	Action to Take	Outcome
What were you doing or thinking?	What were you feeling? 1-10	What went through your mind?	#1 jump to conclusions; #2 over-generalize; #3 either/or	What's the evidence? What's an alternative explanation? So what?	How can you test this out or improve the situation?	How do you feel now?

Extended Thought Record

Situation	Feeling	Thoughts	Error	Answers	Action to Take	Outcome
What were you doing or thinking?	What were you feeling? 1-10	What went through your mind?	#1 jump to conclusions; #2 over-generalize; #3 either/or	What's the evidence? What's an alternative explanation? So what?	How can you test this out or improve the situation?	How do you feel now?

Extended Thought Record

Situation	Feeling	Thoughts	Error	Answers	Action to Take	Outcome
What were you doing or thinking?	What were you feeling? 1-10	What went through your mind?	#1 jump to conclusions; #2 over-generalize; #3 either/or	What's the evidence? What's an alternative explanation? So what?	How can you test this out or improve the situation?	How do you feel now?

Action Schedule

Note: Grade activities M for Mastery and P for Pleasure

	Monday	Tuesday	Wednesday	Thursday	Friday	Saturday	Sunday
9–10							
10–11							
11–12							
12–1							
1–2							
2–3							
3–4							
4–5							
5–6							
6–7							
7–8							
8–12							

Depression Questionnaire

Choose a number from the scale below to show how much you are troubled by each problem listed. Write the number in the blank.

0	1	2	3	4	5	6	7	8
Hardly at all		Slightly troublesome		Definitely troublesome		Markedly troublesome		Very severely troublesome

_____ 1. Feeling miserable, empty, or depressed

_____ 2. Feeling bad about yourself

_____ 3. Feeling discouraged or hopeless about the future

_____ 4. Automatic negative thoughts coming into your mind

_____ 5. Feeling bad or discouraged about your life

_____ 6. Other feelings (describe) _____

_____ 7. How would you rate the present state of your depression symptoms on the scale below? Please circle one number between 0 and 8.

0	1	2	3	4	5	6	7	8
No symptoms present		Slightly disturbing/ not really disturbing		Definitely disturbing/ disabling		Markedly disturbing/ disabling		Very severely disturbing/ disabling

Weekly Practice Record

Goals for Week: Date:

1.

2.

3.

MON	TUES	WED	THUR	FRI	SAT	SUN

Session 8

Correcting Faulty Beliefs

The Power of Your Thoughts

To avoid future depressions, you need to alter the underlying beliefs that predispose you to the disorder. The near compulsion to give yourself and others negative explanations and attributes is a chief feature of depression. Many of the symptoms, such as hopelessness, rumination, and negativity, are really just thoughts ("Nothing matters. Why should I bother?"; "I've got to figure this out *right now*"; "Everything in my life is a disappointment"). These thoughts, which are always about you, isolate you from others, limit and disable you, cutting you off from participating in life.

Normally, you oscillate between feeling relatively stable and relatively unstable. Depression is an extreme state of instability. Being depressed means that you've lost your psychological balance. You then make up negative narratives to give you a sense of control and a way to deal with the uncertainty in your unbalanced life. Your need to feel in control overrides everything, even common sense or the desire to be happy.

Negative Bias

A troubled mind automatically looks for negative explanations. When dysfunctional beliefs from childhood become activated, you tell yourself that you were always a loser and will always be one. You tend to exaggerate the extent of your problems and your role in bringing them about, and these thoughts seem familiar and right. Whatever comes to your mind most easily (whether true or not), you judge as the most probable and true.

Beliefs and Negative Thoughts

Automatic thoughts are generated from your belief systems—beliefs such as "I'm responsible for everyone"; "Unless I'm beautiful I'm nothing"; "I'm stupid and always will be." You can use the same methods that you used to identify automatic thoughts to identify your underlying beliefs and then use the same methods to alter these beliefs. After you have been able to identify what you believe, you can trace automatic thoughts back to the beliefs and then look for more realistic ways of seeing yourself and the world.

The brain is prewired to adopt rules or beliefs. Beliefs help us survive, make sense out of life, select and reach goals, and evaluate and adjust our behavior. Beliefs give meaning to life by providing consistency. Some beliefs work for us, others don't.

When you are depressed, you have an opportunity to see the deeply ingrained beliefs that predispose you to depression. When you fully identify with a belief, it can be difficult to see and accept it as maladaptive and false. We usually can more easily spot extreme beliefs in others than in ourselves.

Early Learning

Your core beliefs revolve around important issues such as love, health, achievement, attractiveness, social and career positions. The beliefs stay in the background, although they may cause you daily stress.

Generally, you picked up your extreme beliefs early in life. For example, if you experienced major losses as a child, you may have developed the belief, "I need to be loved to feel safe."

When, as a child, you experienced an actual or perceived loss in a vulnerable area, a significant loss later in life can energize that deep belief and bring old feelings to the surface. You may, for example, have the latent belief, "I need to be loved to be worthwhile." Then, when a relationship breaks up, that experience energizes the belief, and your dominant thought becomes, "I'm unworthy because I'm rejected." These thoughts naturally depress you, and the more you continue to tell yourself how unlovable you are.

Your thoughts serve to confirm and validate your fixed belief. The thoughts may vary in content, but they usually revolve around one fixed theme. Here are some common beliefs:

- "I am a failure."

- "I am unlovable."

- "I am a victim."

- "I am not good enough."

- "I am an outsider."

- "I am flawed."

- "I am a bad person."

- "I am unlucky."

- "I am untrustworthy."

- "I am doomed."

Your negative beliefs may be listed above, or they may be unique to you. Whatever your beliefs, they are self-fulfilling. If, for example, your belief is "I am an outsider," you will repeatedly tell yourself, "I don't belong," and act in ways that cause you to feel like an outsider.

Find the Belief

It's important for you to become aware of the specific belief or beliefs that predispose you to depression. Beliefs are not something that you directly tell yourself, but are silent assumptions. In this sense, they are nonconscious. Your negative thoughts about yourself, the world, and your future come from your beliefs. Your negative thoughts indicate what your beliefs are.

Look for themes in your thoughts. Notice patterns and keywords. When you are unusually happy, try to determine what belief you're operating from. Pay particular attention to what you tell yourself you think you need but can't have right now ("I need to find someone, but I can't find anyone").

If you still have trouble identifying your beliefs, look at how you view others. You project your beliefs onto others, so look for what you admire or disdain in others. Once you uncover a belief, don't be afraid to acknowledge and accept the belief You are only accepting a concept already in place. By accepting a belief, you begin to loosen the hold it has over you. Through acceptance, you take the power away from the belief.

Choice

As mentioned earlier, choice is a more useful concept than change. Rather than try to change your beliefs, choose a middle or moderate position ("I would like to be loved, but I don't need to be"). Your attempts to change beliefs can actually strengthen them. If you have a negative view of yourself and try to overpower this with a positive view, you'll reinforce the negative ("Who but a loser would try to convince himself that he's a winner?").

Your extreme positive beliefs can cause as much trouble as your negative beliefs. You may tell yourself what you "should do," "must do," "need to do," and "have no choice about." No one likes to be told what to do, even if it's by themselves.

When you give yourself absolute imperatives, you become anxious, frustrated, and discouraged. Try using more flexible and moderate requests of yourself. Remember, needs are arbitrary. There is no absolute way you need to lead your life.

You can certainly use helpful guidelines, such as "treat other people well," but once this becomes an absolute need, you create an opposite motivation. Once you clarify and accept underlying, conflicting beliefs and choose what you want, you can move to a deeper level of understanding that helps prevent future depression.

Take Action

You strengthen any thought or belief that you act on. If you believe you need others to like you and therefore try to impress them, you reinforce the idea that you're not innately likable. By taking action on what needs to be done to get what you want, rather than on impressing others, you weaken the belief. For example, if you want to give a good speech, focus on the content of the speech, not on what others will think of the speech. If you feel compelled to be with others, spend time alone. If you think you need to be accepted, go someplace where you don't feel readily accepted. When you get involved in action that contradicts your belief, you can determine whether the evidence supports your belief. Be prepared for some short-term discomfort, because you'll be in a situation that challenges your belief; however, if you stay with it, the belief will naturally dissolve on its own.

Question the Belief

Questions weaken beliefs. You don't have to answer the question, just raise it. The answer will come on its own. Here are some questions that may help you challenge some beliefs:

- "Where is the evidence that I need to be loved?"
- "Do my bad feelings come from thinking I need to prove I'm good enough?"
- "Do I really need to belong before I can feel whole and complete?"
- "Am I taking the need to be special out of context?"
- "Do I honestly need to be famous?"
- "Is there a real source of my need to belong, or is it just a thought?"
- "Am I confusing the low probability that I need validation with a high probability that I don't?"
- "Am I confusing my present with a past belief that I needed to be important?"
- "Is there a real need to be in control when I consider the big picture?"
- "Is getting the love I demand good for me in the long run?"
- "Is the belief, 'I need to be strong,' undermining my self-esteem?"
- "Is the need to be secure a fantasy?"

Clarification of Beliefs

It's important to clarify your dysfunctional beliefs. You can clarify the belief in many ways: self-reflection, being in the present, monitoring physical and mental processes, widening your circle of interactions, and approaching what you fear.

With clarification, questions are more important than answers. Unlike analysis, the aim for clarification is to investigate rather than interpret your belief—to see more and think less. Questions eventually start to answer themselves. Clarification, if carried through, allows you to abandon outdated world views and discover what is truly important to you.

To clarify, all you have to do is ask yourself questions and reflect back on what you observe. Once you understand the nature of beliefs, they often dissolve by themselves. It is important to stay open to the possibility that your beliefs may be the opposite of what you consciously think.

You can always further clarify a belief. When you first look at what's going on deep down, you will focus on your personal concerns. Continue to clarify until there is a shift to a more general look at the belief.

Homework

The homework for session 8 is as follows:

1. Do one thought record on a situation generated by your central belief.

2. Practice noting and dropping thoughts associated with your central belief.

Extended Thought Record

Situation	Feeling	Thoughts	Error	Answers	Action to Take	Outcome
What were you doing or thinking?	What were you feeling? 1-10	What went through your mind?	#1 jump to conclusions; #2 over-generalize; #3 either/or	What's the evidence? What's an alternative explanation? So what?	How can you test this out or improve the situation?	How do you feel now?

Extended Thought Record

Situation	Feeling	Thoughts	Error	Answers	Action to Take	Outcome
What were you doing or thinking?	What were you feeling? 1-10	What went through your mind?	#1 jump to conclusions; #2 over-generalize; #3 either/or	What's the evidence? What's an alternative explanation? So what?	How can you test this out or improve the situation?	How do you feel now?

Extended Thought Record

Situation	Feeling	Thoughts	Error	Answers	Action to Take	Outcome
What were you doing or thinking?	What were you feeling? 1-10	What went through your mind?	#1 jump to conclusions; #2 over-generalize; #3 either/or	What's the evidence? What's an alternative explanation? So what?	How can you test this out or improve the situation?	How do you feel now?

Extended Thought Record

Situation	Feeling	Thoughts	Error	Answers	Action to Take	Outcome
What were you doing or thinking?	What were you feeling? 1-10	What went through your mind?	#1 jump to conclusions; #2 over-generalize; #3 either/or	What's the evidence? What's an alternative explanation? So what?	How can you test this out or improve the situation?	How do you feel now?

Extended Thought Record

Situation	Feeling	Thoughts	Error	Answers	Action to Take	Outcome
What were you doing or thinking?	What were you feeling? 1-10	What went through your mind?	#1 jump to conclusions; #2 over-generalize; #3 either/or	What's the evidence? What's an alternative explanation? So what?	How can you test this out or improve the situation?	How do you feel now?

Extended Thought Record

Situation	Feeling	Thoughts	Error	Answers	Action to Take	Outcome
What were you doing or thinking?	What were you feeling? 1-10	What went through your mind?	#1 jump to conclusions; #2 over-generalize; #3 either/or	What's the evidence? What's an alternative explanation? So what?	How can you test this out or improve the situation?	How do you feel now?

Extended Thought Record

Situation	Feeling	Thoughts	Error	Answers	Action to Take	Outcome
What were you doing or thinking?	What were you feeling? 1-10	What went through your mind?	#1 jump to conclusions; #2 over-generalize; #3 either/or	What's the evidence? What's an alternative explanation? So what?	How can you test this out or improve the situation?	How do you feel now?

Extended Thought Record

Situation	Feeling	Thoughts	Error	Answers	Action to Take	Outcome
What were you doing or thinking?	What were you feeling? 1-10	What went through your mind?	#1 jump to conclusions; #2 over-generalize; #3 either/or	What's the evidence? What's an alternative explanation? So what?	How can you test this out or improve the situation?	How do you feel now?

Extended Thought Record

Situation	Feeling	Thoughts	Error	Answers	Action to Take	Outcome
What were you doing or thinking?	What were you feeling? 1-10	What went through your mind?	#1 jump to conclusions; #2 over-generalize; #3 either/or	What's the evidence? What's an alternative explanation? So what?	How can you test this out or improve the situation?	How do you feel now?

Extended Thought Record

Situation	Feeling	Thoughts	Error	Answers	Action to Take	Outcome
What were you doing or thinking?	What were you feeling? 1-10	What went through your mind?	#1 jump to conclusions; #2 over-generalize; #3 either/or	What's the evidence? What's an alternative explanation? So what?	How can you test this out or improve the situation?	How do you feel now?

Action Schedule

Note: Grade activities M for Mastery and P for Pleasure

	Monday	Tuesday	Wednesday	Thursday	Friday	Saturday	Sunday
9–10							
10–11							
11–12							
12–1							
1–2							
2–3							
3–4							
4–5							
5–6							
6–7							
7–8							
8–12							

Depression Questionnaire

Choose a number from the scale below to show how much you are troubled by each problem listed. Write the number in the blank.

0	1	2	3	4	5	6	7	8
Hardly at all		Slightly troublesome		Definitely troublesome		Markedly troublesome		Very severely troublesome

_____ 1. Feeling miserable, empty, or depressed

_____ 2. Feeling bad about yourself

_____ 3. Feeling discouraged or hopeless about the future

_____ 4. Automatic negative thoughts coming into your mind

_____ 5. Feeling bad or discouraged about your life

_____ 6. Other feelings (describe) _____

_____ 7. How would you rate the present state of your depression symptoms on the scale below? Please circle one number between 0 and 8.

0	1	2	3	4	5	6	7	8
No symptoms present		Slightly disturbing/ not really disturbing		Definitely disturbing/ disabling		Markedly disturbing/ disabling		Very severely disturbing/ disabling

Weekly Practice Record

Goals for Week: Date:

1.

2.

3.

MON	TUES	WED	THUR	FRI	SAT	SUN

Session 9

Preparing for Therapy Completion

Your Progress

The first order of business in this session is to evaluate how you are doing with therapy. As in the previous session, your therapist will assist you to work through any possible obstacles that may have come up.

You and your therapist will also decide whether it is useful to continue therapy beyond ten sessions. If your insurance or personal resources allow for this, it may be appropriate to continue with therapy for up to fifteen to twenty sessions. One reason you may want to continue with therapy is if you're still experiencing some depression. Another reason for extending therapy may be to address personality or interpersonal issues that are interfering with your progress.

If your insurance or personal resources do not permit you to continue past ten therapy sessions, your therapist will help you to plan how to continue on your own. In many cases, your therapist will arrange for a follow-up session one or two months after the tenth session to evaluate your overall progress. Also, your therapist can be available to you by phone should you encounter problems or obstacles or have a setback. Your therapist's responsibility is to support you until you reach your goal, whether it's mastery of your thoughts and feelings, or simply coping more ably with your depression.

Note and Replace with Good Feelings

You may recall your therapist talking about "overthinking," which is incessant self-talk that distracts you from really experiencing your feelings and seeing your beliefs. It's important that you understand that the best way to modify beliefs is to stop the self-talk that marks them.

Once the endless loop of overthinking starts up, your focus turns inward and you're no longer seeing facts objectively. Overthinking misdirects you to see through the prism of your belief system and miss much of reality. Strive to quiet down you mind, not speed it up with racing dialogue.

Rather than help you figure things out, overthinking makes you more vulnerable. Problems can be compounded when you get caught up in self-talk, because you become completely internally focused when you should be paying attention to what is going on with the problem. The distraction of overthinking makes the misinterpretation of events much more likely, and misinterpretations feed faulty evidence to dysfunctional beliefs.

Your energy goes where you focus. Your mind has a self-limited capacity for processing information. You can fill this capacity with overthinking or you can take in reality and get things done. The good news is that once you understand the futility of self-talk, you will start to dismiss overthinking as soon as you catch it.

Points to Keep in Mind

Here are some key points about overthinking that you can keep in mind. When you find yourself slipping into the merry-go-round of overthinking, you can look at this list to help yourself snap out of it.

- Once overthinking starts up, your focus turns inward and you stop seeing the facts objectively.

- With overthinking, you see through your belief system and miss many of the facts.

- Overthinking can become an endless loop. Strive to quiet down the mind, not speed it up with racing dialogue.

- You may believe thinking helps you, but it actually makes you more vulnerable. Problems can become compounded because you get caught up in self-talk instead of paying attention to what is actually going on. This distraction makes the misinterpretation of events much more likely, giving you more faulty evidence to feed your dysfunctional beliefs.

- Where you focus is where your energy goes. So, if your focus is constantly on problems and negative events, you will put your energy into this overthinking and have less energy for taking necessary and truly helpful action.

- The mind has a self-limited capacity for processing information. You can fill this capacity with overthinking or, on the other hand, with taking in reality.

- Once you understand the futility of self-talk, you will start to dismiss it as soon as you catch it.

Homework

Homework for session 9 is as follows:

1. Do at least one thought record a day on your central dysfunctional belief.

2. Practice noting and dropping thoughts generated by your belief.

3. Complete the Program Satisfaction Questionnaire found at the end of this session. Bring the completed form to your next session.

Extended Thought Record

Situation	Feeling	Thoughts	Error	Answers	Action to Take	Outcome
What were you doing or thinking?	What were you feeling? 1-10	What went through your mind?	#1 jump to conclusions; #2 over-generalize; #3 either/or	What's the evidence? What's an alternative explanation? So what?	How can you test this out or improve the situation?	How do you feel now?

Extended Thought Record

Situation	Feeling	Thoughts	Error	Answers	Action to Take	Outcome
What were you doing or thinking?	What were you feeling? 1-10	What went through your mind?	#1 jump to conclusions; #2 over-generalize; #3 either/or	What's the evidence? What's an alternative explanation? So what?	How can you test this out or improve the situation?	How do you feel now?

Extended Thought Record

Situation	Feeling	Thoughts	Error	Answers	Action to Take	Outcome
What were you doing or thinking?	What were you feeling? 1-10	What went through your mind?	#1 jump to conclusions; #2 over-generalize; #3 either/or	What's the evidence? What's an alternative explanation? So what?	How can you test this out or improve the situation?	How do you feel now?

Extended Thought Record

Situation	Feeling	Thoughts	Error		Answers	Action to Take	Outcome
What were you doing or thinking?	What were you feeling? 1-10	What went through your mind?	#1 jump to conclusions; #2 over-generalize; #3 either/or		What's the evidence? What's an alternative explanation? So what?	How can you test this out or improve the situation?	How do you feel now?

Extended Thought Record

Situation	Feeling	Thoughts	Error	Answers	Action to Take	Outcome
What were you doing or thinking?	What were you feeling? 1-10	What went through your mind?	#1 jump to conclusions; #2 over-generalize; #3 either/or	What's the evidence? What's an alternative explanation? So what?	How can you test this out or improve the situation?	How do you feel now?

Extended Thought Record

Situation	Feeling	Thoughts	Error	Answers	Action to Take	Outcome
What were you doing or thinking?	What were you feeling? 1-10	What went through your mind?	#1 jump to conclusions; #2 over-generalize; #3 either/or	What's the evidence? What's an alternative explanation? So what?	How can you test this out or improve the situation?	How do you feel now?

Extended Thought Record

Situation	Feeling	Thoughts	Error	Answers	Action to Take	Outcome
What were you doing or thinking?	What were you feeling? 1-10	What went through your mind?	#1 jump to conclusions; #2 over-generalize; #3 either/or	What's the evidence? What's an alternative explanation? So what?	How can you test this out or improve the situation?	How do you feel now?

Extended Thought Record

Situation	Feeling	Thoughts	Error	Answers	Action to Take	Outcome
What were you doing or thinking?	What were you feeling? 1-10	What went through your mind?	#1 jump to conclusions; #2 over-generalize; #3 either/or	What's the evidence? What's an alternative explanation? So what?	How can you test this out or improve the situation?	How do you feel now?

Extended Thought Record

Situation	Feeling	Thoughts	Error	Answers	Action to Take	Outcome
What were you doing or thinking?	What were you feeling? 1-10	What went through your mind?	#1 jump to conclusions; #2 over-generalize; #3 either/or	What's the evidence? What's an alternative explanation? So what?	How can you test this out or improve the situation?	How do you feel now?

Extended Thought Record

Situation	Feeling	Thoughts	Error	Answers	Action to Take	Outcome
What were you doing or thinking?	What were you feeling? 1-10	What went through your mind?	#1 jump to conclusions; #2 over-generalize; #3 either/or	What's the evidence? What's an alternative explanation? So what?	How can you test this out or improve the situation?	How do you feel now?

Action Schedule

Note: Grade activities M for Mastery and P for Pleasure

	Monday	Tuesday	Wednesday	Thursday	Friday	Saturday	Sunday
9–10							
10–11							
11–12							
12–1							
1–2							
2–3							
3–4							
4–5							
5–6							
6–7							
7–8							
8–12							

Depression Questionnaire

Choose a number from the scale below to show how much you are troubled by each problem listed. Write the number in the blank.

0	1	2	3	4	5	6	7	8
Hardly at all		Slightly troublesome		Definitely troublesome		Markedly troublesome		Very severely troublesome

_____ 1. Feeling miserable, empty, or depressed

_____ 2. Feeling bad about yourself

_____ 3. Feeling discouraged or hopeless about the future

_____ 4. Automatic negative thoughts coming into your mind

_____ 5. Feeling bad or discouraged about your life

_____ 6. Other feelings (describe) _____

_____ 7. How would you rate the present state of your depression symptoms on the scale below? Please circle one number between 0 and 8.

0	1	2	3	4	5	6	7	8
No symptoms present		Slightly disturbing/ not really disturbing		Definitely disturbing/ disabling		Markedly disturbing/ disabling		Very severely disturbing/ disabling

Weekly Practice Record

Goals for Week: Date:

1.

2.

3.

MON	TUES	WED	THUR	FRI	SAT	SUN

Program Satisfaction Questionnaire (PSQ)

Please evaluate the therapy program you have just completed by answering the following questions. Circle the number that best reflects your opinion. Your honest answer, whether positive or negative, will give us feedback to make the program better.

1. How effective was the therapy program in helping you with your problem?

   1   2   3   4   5   6   7
   Not effective   *Moderately effective*   *Extremely effective*

2. How helpful were the homework and exercises in this therapy program?

   1   2   3   4   5   6   7
   Not helpful   *Moderately helpful*   *Extremely helpful*

3. Were the skills you learned in this therapy program useful for coping with your problem?

   1   2   3   4   5   6   7
   Not useful   *Moderately useful*   *Extremely useful*

4. Overall, how would you rate the quality of this therapy?

   1   2   3   4   5   6   7
   High quality   *Moderate Quality*   *Low Quality*

5. If someone with a similar problem to yours asked for recommendations, how would you describe the usefulness of this therapy program?

   1   2   3   4   5   6   7
   Not useful   *Moderately useful*   *Extremely useful*

6. If you could go back to remake your decision about this therapy program, would you do it again?

   1   2   3   4   5   6   7
   No, definitely   *Uncertain*   *Yes, definitely*

7. How successfully were your goals met by this therapy program?

   1   2   3   4   5   6   7
   Goals met   *Moderately successful*   *Goals not met*
                              with goals

8. How would you rate your improvement in the symptoms that concerned you most?

   1   2   3   4   5   6   7
   Extremely improved   *Moderately improved*   *Not improved*

Session 10

Final Session

Perhaps this is your final session. If so, the session will focus on three themes: 1) summarizing your progress to date, 2) discussing strategies for relapse prevention, and 3) achieving closure. You and your therapist will discuss your progress up to this point. Are you satisfied with how far you've come? Are you satisfied with therapy in general—or is there something you wish had happened that didn't? Are you willing to make a commitment following the final therapy session to continue using the activity schedule and thought record until you reach your goal? Would you like to be able to call your therapist to report progress or any obstacles that arise? Would you like to have a follow-up session in one or two months?

There are two things to be aware of in minimizing the prospect of relapse following therapy. First, be aware of any resistance to practicing the skills that may arise when you don't have the support of weekly therapy sessions. It's important to notice any procrastination or delay in using them—the proverbial "I'll do it tomorrow." If this gets to be a problem, be willing to call your therapist.

When you and your therapist have finished discussing your satisfaction level with regard to the therapy and how to minimize the prospect of relapse, it's time to bring therapy to a close. You and your therapist will talk about any feelings that come up around having to end the therapy. This is unlikely to be your final contact with your therapist, since arrangements for a follow-up session and/or continuing support by phone are already in place.

Extended Thought Record

Situation	Feeling	Thoughts	Error	Answers	Action to Take	Outcome
What were you doing or thinking?	What were you feeling? 1-10	What went through your mind?	#1 jump to conclusions; #2 over-generalize; #3 either/or	What's the evidence? What's an alternative explanation? So what?	How can you test this out or improve the situation?	How do you feel now?

Extended Thought Record

Situation	Feeling	Thoughts	Error	Answers	Action to Take	Outcome
What were you doing or thinking?	What were you feeling? 1-10	What went through your mind?	#1 jump to conclusions; #2 over-generalize; #3 either/or	What's the evidence? What's an alternative explanation? So what?	How can you test this out or improve the situation?	How do you feel now?

Extended Thought Record

Situation	Feeling	Thoughts	Error	Answers	Action to Take	Outcome
What were you doing or thinking?	What were you feeling? 1-10	What went through your mind?	#1 jump to conclusions; #2 over-generalize; #3 either/or	What's the evidence? What's an alternative explanation? So what?	How can you test this out or improve the situation?	How do you feel now?

Extended Thought Record

Situation	Feeling	Thoughts	Error	Answers	Action to Take	Outcome
What were you doing or thinking?	What were you feeling? 1-10	What went through your mind?	#1 jump to conclusions; #2 over-generalize; #3 either/or	What's the evidence? What's an alternative explanation? So what?	How can you test this out or improve the situation?	How do you feel now?

Extended Thought Record

Situation	Feeling	Thoughts	Error	Answers	Action to Take	Outcome
What were you doing or thinking?	What were you feeling? 1-10	What went through your mind?	#1 jump to conclusions; #2 over-generalize; #3 either/or	What's the evidence? What's an alternative explanation? So what?	How can you test this out or improve the situation?	How do you feel now?

Extended Thought Record

Situation	Feeling	Thoughts	Error	Answers	Action to Take	Outcome
What were you doing or thinking?	What were you feeling? 1-10	What went through your mind?	#1 jump to conclusions; #2 over-generalize; #3 either/or	What's the evidence? What's an alternative explanation? So what?	How can you test this out or improve the situation?	How do you feel now?

Extended Thought Record

Situation	Feeling	Thoughts	Error	Answers	Action to Take	Outcome
What were you doing or thinking?	What were you feeling? 1-10	What went through your mind?	#1 jump to conclusions; #2 over-generalize; #3 either/or	What's the evidence? What's an alternative explanation? So what?	How can you test this out or improve the situation?	How do you feel now?

Extended Thought Record

Situation	Feeling	Thoughts	Error	Answers	Action to Take	Outcome
What were you doing or thinking?	What were you feeling? 1-10	What went through your mind?	#1 jump to conclusions; #2 over-generalize; #3 either/or	What's the evidence? What's an alternative explanation? So what?	How can you test this out or improve the situation?	How do you feel now?

Extended Thought Record

Situation	Feeling	Thoughts	Error	Answers	Action to Take	Outcome
What were you doing or thinking?	What were you feeling? 1-10	What went through your mind?	#1 jump to conclusions; #2 over-generalize; #3 either/or	What's the evidence? What's an alternative explanation? So what?	How can you test this out or improve the situation?	How do you feel now?

Extended Thought Record

Situation	Feeling	Thoughts	Error	Answers	Action to Take	Outcome
What were you doing or thinking?	What were you feeling? 1-10	What went through your mind?	#1 jump to conclusions; #2 over-generalize; #3 either/or	What's the evidence? What's an alternative explanation? So what?	How can you test this out or improve the situation?	How do you feel now?

Action Schedule

Note: Grade activities M for Mastery and P for Pleasure

	Monday	Tuesday	Wednesday	Thursday	Friday	Saturday	Sunday
9–10							
10–11							
11–12							
12–1							
1–2							
2–3							
3–4							
4–5							
5–6							
6–7							
7–8							
8–12							

Depression Questionnaire

Choose a number from the scale below to show how much you are troubled by each problem listed. Write the number in the blank.

0	1	2	3	4	5	6	7	8
Hardly at all		Slightly troublesome		Definitely troublesome		Markedly troublesome		Very severely troublesome

_____ 1. Feeling miserable, empty, or depressed

_____ 2. Feeling bad about yourself

_____ 3. Feeling discouraged or hopeless about the future

_____ 4. Automatic negative thoughts coming into your mind

_____ 5. Feeling bad or discouraged about your life

_____ 6. Other feelings (describe) _____

_____ 7. How would you rate the present state of your depression symptoms on the scale below? Please circle one number between 0 and 8.

0	1	2	3	4	5	6	7	8
No symptoms present		Slightly disturbing/ not really disturbing		Definitely disturbing/ disabling		Markedly disturbing/ disabling		Very severely disturbing/ disabling

Weekly Practice Record

Goals for Week: Date:

1.

2.

3.

MON	TUES	WED	THUR	FRI	SAT	SUN

Center for Epidemiologic Studies Depressed Mood Scale (CES-D)

Using the scale below, indicate the number which best describes how often you felt, or behaved this way DURING THE PAST WEEK.

0 = Rarely or none of the time (less than 1 time)

1 = Some or a little of the time (1-2 days)

2 = Occasionally or a moderate amount of time (3-4 days)

3 = Most or all of the time (5-7 days)

DURING THE PAST WEEK

_____ 1. I was bothered by things that usually don't bother me.

_____ 2. I did not feel like eating; my appetite was poor.

_____ 3. I felt that I could not shake off the blues even with help from my family or friends.

_____ 4. I felt that I was just as good as other people.

_____ 5. I had trouble keeping my mind on what I was doing.

_____ 6. I felt depressed.

_____ 7. I felt that everything I did was an effort.

_____ 8. I felt hopeful about the future.

_____ 9. I thought my life had been a failure.

_____ 10. I felt fearful.

_____ 11. My sleep was restless.

_____ 12. I was happy.

_____ 13. I talked less than usual.

_____ 14. I felt lonely.

_____ 15. People were unfriendly.

_____ 16. I enjoyed life.

_____ 17. I had crying spells.

_____ 18. I felt sad.

_____ 19. I felt that people dislike me.

_____ 20. I could not get "going."

Further Reading

Beck, Aaron T., and Gary Emery. 1981. *Anxiety Disorders and Phobias: A Cognitive Perspective*. New York: Basic Books.

Beck, Aaron T., A. John Rush, Brian Shaw, and Gary Emery. 1979. *Cognitive Therapy of Depression*. New York: Guilford Press.

Burns, David. 1981. *Feeling Good*. New York: New American Library.

Emery, Gary. 1988. *Getting Undepressed: How a Woman Can Change Her Life Through Cognitive Therapy*. New York: Touchstone.

Emery, Gary, and James Campbell. 1986. *Rapid Relief from Emotional Distress*. New York: Fawcett Columbine.

Emery, Gary, and Pat Emery. 1990. *The Positive Force: Overcoming Your Resistance to Success*. New York: Signet.

Jamison, K. R. 1999. *Night Falls Fast: Understanding Suicide*. New York: Alfred Knopf.

McKay, Matthew, and Patrick Fanning. 1997. *Thoughts and Feelings*, 2nd ed. Oakland, Calif.: New Harbinger Publications.

Schiffer, F. 1998. *Of Two Minds: The Revolutionary Science of Dual-Brain Psychology*. New York: The Free Press.

Best Practices For Therapy

Each of the protocols in this series presents a session-by-session, research-based treatment plan, including evaluation instruments, sample treatment summaries for use with managed care, handouts, weekly homework, and strategies to use for delivering key information. A client manual is available for each protocol, containing all the materials that the client will need.

ADDITIONAL TITLES NOW AVAILABLE

Overcoming Agoraphobia and Panic Disorder
By Elke Zuercher-White, Ph.D.
Therapist protocol, *item APDP $24.95.*
Client manual. *item APDM $11.95.*
Client pack—set of five client manuals, *item APM5 29.95.*

Overcoming Generalized Anxiety Disorder
By John White, Ph.D.
Therapist protocol, *item GADP, $19.59.*
Client manual, *item GADM, $11.95.*
Client pack—set of five client manuals, *item GAM5 $29.95.*

Overcoming Obsessive-Compulsive Disorder
By Gail Steketee, Ph.D.
Therapist protocol, *item OCDP $24.95.*
Client manual. *item OCDM $15.95.*
Client pack—set of five client manuals, *item OCM5 29.95.*

Overcoming Post-Traumatic Stress Disorder
By Larry Smyth, Ph.D.
Therapist protocol, *item PTSP $24.95.*
Client manual, *item PTSM $11.95.*
Client pack—set of five client manuals, *item PTM5 $29.95.*

Overcoming Specific Phobia
By Edmund J. Bourne, Ph.D.
Therapist protocol, *item POSP $19.95.*
Client manual, *item PHM $9.95.*
Client pack—set of five client manuals, *item PHM5 $24.95.*

Call toll-free 1-800-748-6273 to order. Have your Visa or Mastercard number ready. Or send a check for the titles you want to New Harbinger Publications, 5674 Shattuck Avenue, Oakland, CA 94609. Include $3.80 for the first item and 75¢ for each additional item to cover shipping and handling. (California residents please include appropriate sales tax.) Allow four

Some Other
New Harbinger Titles

The Anxiety & Phobia Workbook, 3rd edition, Item PHO3 $19.95

Beyond Anxiety & Phobia, Item BYAP $19.95

The Self-Nourishment Companion, Item SNC $10.95

The Healing Sorrow Workbook, Item HSW $17.95

The Daily Relaxer, Item DALY $12.95

Stop Controlling Me!, Item SCM $13.95

Lift Your Mood Now, Item LYMN $12.95

An End to Panic, 2nd edition, Item END2 $19.95

Serenity to Go, Item STG $12.95

The Depression Workbook, Item DEP $19.95

The OCD Workbook, Item OCD $18.95

The Anger Control Workbook, Item ACWB $17.95

Flying without Fear, Item FLY $14.95

The Shyness & Social Anxiety Workbook, Item SHYW $15.95

The Relaxation & Stress Reduction Workbook, 5th edition, Item RS5 $19.95

Energy Tapping, Item ETAP $14.95

Stop Walking on Eggshells, Item WOE $14.95

Angry All the Time, Item ALL 12.95

Living without Procrastination, Item $12.95

Hypnosis for Change, 3rd edition, Item HYP3 $16.95

Don't Take it Personally, Item DOTA $15.95

Toxic Coworkers, Item TOXC $13.95

Letting Go of Anger, Item LET $13.95

Call **toll free, 1-800-748-6273,** or log on to our online bookstore at **www.newharbinger.com** to order. Have your Visa or Mastercard number ready. Or send a check for the titles you want to New Harbinger Publications, Inc., 5674 Shattuck Ave., Oakland, CA 94609. Include $4.50 for the first book and 75¢ for each additional book, to cover shipping and handling. (California residents please include appropriate sales tax.) Allow two to five weeks for delivery.

Prices subject to change without notice.